Rocky Harbors

TAKING STOCK OF THE MIDDLE EAST IN 2015

EDITOR
Jon B. Alterman

CONTRIBUTORS
Carolyn Barnett
Stephen D. Biddle
Farideh Farhi
Haim Malka
John McLaughlin
Ghaith al-Omari
Roger Owen
Paul Salem

CSIS | CENTER FOR STRATEGIC & INTERNATIONAL STUDIES

A Report of the CSIS Middle East Program
2015

About CSIS

For over 50 years, the Center for Strategic and International Studies (CSIS) has worked to develop solutions to the world's greatest policy challenges. Today, CSIS scholars are providing strategic insights and bipartisan policy solutions to help decisionmakers chart a course toward a better world.

CSIS is a nonprofit organization headquartered in Washington, D.C. The Center's 220 full-time staff and large network of affiliated scholars conduct research and analysis and develop policy initiatives that look into the future and anticipate change.

Founded at the height of the Cold War by David M. Abshire and Admiral Arleigh Burke, CSIS was dedicated to finding ways to sustain American prominence and prosperity as a force for good in the world. Since 1962, CSIS has become one of the world's preeminent international institutions focused on defense and security; regional stability; and transnational challenges ranging from energy and climate to global health and economic integration.

Former U.S. senator Sam Nunn has chaired the CSIS Board of Trustees since 1999. Former deputy secretary of defense John J. Hamre became the Center's president and chief executive officer in 2000.

ISBN: 978-1-4422-4096-4 (pb); 978-1-4422-4097-1 (eBook)

Center for Strategic & International Studies
1616 Rhode Island Avenue NW
Washington, DC 20036
202-887-0200 | **www.csis.org**

Rowman & Littlefield
4501 Forbes Boulevard
Lanham, MD 20706
301- 459- 3366 | **www.rowman.com**

Table of Contents

1 Seeking Harbors in the Storm

JON B. ALTERMAN

Many things in life have clear beginnings, middles, and ends. Games, concerts, plays, and books all start differently, they follow different paths, and they have different endings, but there is no escaping the iron logic of their architecture. Lives themselves are the same way. Circumstances of birth and death may differ, and trajectories may vary, but at some point the end comes, and it can be judged.

The political life of a country is different. It rarely has a clear beginning or a clear end. Individuals come and go, but the nation to which they belong both precedes and succeeds them. Still, individuals and groups can shift the course of politics, giving them a kind of immortality.

It was a desire to change the course of history that drove the passions of the Arab uprisings in 2011. Millions poured into the streets. Billions watched, admired the courage, and shared the hope of those willing to risk their lives in the early days.

The rush to call the uprisings "revolutions," and even more to describe the regional phenomenon as an "Arab Spring," seems naïve in retrospect. Both terms presumed an inevitable outcome of political action: more representative—and one would hope, more effective—government in the Arab world, affecting not only the revolutionary republics of North Africa and the Levant but spreading to the region's monarchies as well. In retrospect, we see that the belief that Arab politics were opening up in a fundamental way was premature, and some might even argue, misguided.

This volume comes at a time of profound uncertainty about the future of political life in the Middle East. Where some see an interregnum in efforts by younger and more connected populations to push for inclusion, others see a region coming to its senses after a moment of irrational exuberance. Some see a state system that is increasingly weary, while others see a state system fortified by the knowledge that its demise would bring chaos. The events of the last five years suggest that regional politics are interconnected, but the manner of their interconnections is a source of constant surprise. While it is impossible to predict their direction, the last five years have helped us understand some of the key variables, and what to notice.

The sheer unpredictability of Tunisia's course—its sudden and surprising revolution in 2011, and its similarly sudden turn away from Islamist governance in 2014—is a reminder of just how dynamic politics can be. The Islamist Ennahda Party seemed unstoppable in the early days of Tunisia's political transition, and the ancien régime had been completely discredited. Yet, Ennahda soon stumbled. In part the group overreached, and in part it failed to rein in some of Tunisia's Islamist radicals. Violence spiked, and the economy stayed flat. Ultimately, Ennahda eroded its own support, and it helped its opposition consolidate. By December 2014 it was firmly in the minority, and the unthinkable had occurred: elderly personalities from the Zine el-Abidine Ben Ali period had won democratic elections and were back in control.

Egypt followed a similar path. The Muslim Brotherhood misread its mandate, substituting one authoritarian regime for another. It replaced minimally competent regime apparatchiks with completely incompetent party functionaries, alienating both those whom it had displaced as well as those who had hoped that the Brotherhood's reputation for competence and probity would deliver better governance. In addition, the Brotherhood failed in its approach to Egypt's military, the country's most trusted and most effective institution. The Brotherhood did not try to crush the organization, nor was it able to co-opt it, but instead hinted that it was winning over the military from within. In so doing, the Brotherhood made a costly miscalculation that resulted with another retired general in the presidential palace, and much of the Brotherhood leadership in jail or in exile.

And for all of the despair that activists have felt in Tunisia and Egypt, these are the bright spots. Bahrain has become only more polarized, with political participation vanishing among the majority Shi'ite population. The governments of Syria, Iraq, Libya, and Yemen have lost control over vast swaths of their territory. While Tunisia's and Egypt's processes at least hold out the possibility of progress, the others appear set for years of conflict.

For the publics who were inspired by politics four years ago, resignation and despair have set in. Many liberal activists have retreated from public space, or they have lined up behind authoritarian governments. After remarkable expressions of unity that brought together young and old, rich and poor, religious and secular in the public squares of the Arab world, Arab societies are increasingly polarized and increasingly paranoid. Reports have emerged from Egypt of vigilante efforts to enforce order. One activist reported the story of a woman who sought to entrap a fellow bus passenger into statements critical of the government and then sought his arrest for extremism.[1] A few weeks later, a prominent French journalist was detained by police in Cairo after being overheard discussing politics with Egyptian colleagues. An Egyptian woman was apparently offended by his analysis, shouted "You want to destroy the country!" and summoned the police.[2] Meanwhile, a survey in Egypt in September 2014 suggested a deep rift in Egyptian society. When asked "Has the role of the Muslim Brotherhood been positive or negative in Egypt?" 43 percent of Egyptians responded "positive" and 44 percent responded "negative."[3]

> *After seeming to feel some despair early in the 2011, officials in Arab governments seem to feel renewed resolve.*

After seeming to feel some despair early in 2011, officials in Arab governments seem to feel renewed resolve. At the same time, they are far from feeling secure. In part, they worry that the array of conflicts in the Middle East provides a wealth of ungoverned space in which young men can radicalize, network, and train. Almost 20,000 have left their countries to fight in Iraq, Syria, and beyond.[4] No one really knows what is happening in the Libyan desert, and the Sinai is shot through with smugglers and brigands who are severely testing the mettle of the Egyptian military. Millions of refugees have crowded into small countries such as Jordan and

---

1. Belal Fadl, "Egypt: The Nation of Snitches Makes a Comeback," *Mada Masr,* November 9, 2014, http://www.madamasr.com/opinion/politics/egypt-nation-snitches-makes-comeback.
2. Alain Gresh, "I Was Arrested for Chatting in a Cairo Café," November 15, 2014, *Al Jazeera,* http://www.aljazeera.com/indepth/opinion/2014/11/i-was-arrested-chatting-cairo-2014111417501295578.html
3. Zogby Research Services, "Today's Middle East: Pressures and Challenges," prepared for the Sir Bani Yas Forum, November 2014, 11, http://b.3cdn.net/aai/a6466ad6476c08d752_bum6b4j6l.pdf.
4. See Nicholas J. Rasmussen (Director, National Counterterrorism Center), "Countering Violent Islamist Extremism: The urgent threat of foreign fighters and homegrown terror," Testimony before House Committee on Homeland Security, February 11, 2015, 1, http://www.odni.gov/files/documents/Newsroom/Testimonies/11%20Feb%20HHSC%20Foreign%20Fighter%20Travel%20Rasmussen%20SFR.pdf.

Lebanon, not only skewing local economies and local demographics, but also introducing extremist elements into these populations who embark on their own radicalization and recruitment efforts.

Yet, for many governments, the foreign fighter problem is a discrete one and a relatively small one. The intelligence services, often in cooperation with Western counterparts, have the experience of the Afghan war under their belts, and they can keep a close eye on individuals they suspect of malfeasance.

The much larger problem for them is the threat they feel from their domestic political opposition, given how quickly that opposition mushroomed in the weeks before Ben Ali fell in Tunisia. Massive crowds quickly overwhelmed both the internal security systems and the uniformed police in many Arab states, often leaving militaries with the uncomfortable options of firing on large groups of unarmed civilians or accepting the failure of sitting governments. Today's governments appear to have concluded that two tactics could have averted the situation: being more aggressive against dissent when it was still widely dispersed, and showing more resolve in the face of protests. The scorecard remains incomplete, but it is hard to think of a president who negotiated with a mass protest movement and is still in office. By contrast, leaders from Bashar al-Assad in Syria to King Hamad in Bahrain were resolute and remain; for those deposed who did not negotiate, such as Muammar el-Qaddafi in Libya, it is unclear if he would have fallen were it not for sustained outside intervention.

Massive crowds quickly overwhelmed both the internal security systems and the uniformed police in many Arab states, often leaving militaries with the uncomfortable options of firing on large groups of unarmed civilians or accepting the failure of sitting governments.

The specific threat that governments worry about most in the current environment is the Muslim Brotherhood, whose actions over the last four years left little doubt about the organization's thirst for political power. Whether Brotherhood politicians would ever voluntarily relinquish power is contested—and Egypt and Tunisia provide contradictory evidence. For rulers throughout the region who see sustaining power as their own existential battle, the Brotherhood's political effectiveness and widespread support is a worrying sign.

The rising focus on the Brotherhood in states as diverse as Egypt, Tunisia, Saudi Arabia, and the United Arab Emirates suggests that the most important battle of 2011 is still raging. That battle is one for authority, which has two components: legitimacy and power. The Brotherhood emphasized its religious credentials to attack the legitimacy of existing governments, questioning both the process through which they came to power and their performance in power. For their part, governments have used their temporal power to undermine the Brotherhood, often rounding up supporters under accusations of terrorism. Meanwhile, governments have unleashed their own attacks on the Brotherhood's religious legitimacy, deploying establishment clerics who undermine the Brotherhood's call to question authority. Salafi groups are interestingly split in this battle. Some see the current confrontation as proof that the departure from their traditional political quietism in 2011 was a mistake. The leadership of several groups, such as the Nour Party in Egypt, appears to be seeking to revive the informal agreements they had with the security services. In some cases, they seem committed to being apolitical, and in others, to be loyal to the government. In either instance, they stand as a religious counterbalance to the Brotherhood. Other salafists appear more sympathetic to the Brotherhood, and they see government steps to sideline it as an effort to impose authoritarian secularism on society.

Liberals, who formed an important core of the opposition to authoritarian rulers, have been put in a difficult position. Their alliance with Islamist groups proved fleeting, and they feared a religious authoritarianism which was even less accommodating and more hostile than the secular authoritarianism of the ancien régime. Many liberals have made their peace with the authoritarianism of existing governments, seeking their protection from Islamists.

Looking forward, there are several variables that will have profound impacts on the direction of Arab society and Arab politics. The first is the growth of information and communications technology. Technology enthusiasts exulted in the impact that social media had on the uprisings of 2011. Twitter, Facebook, and Reddit gave an immediacy to the protests in the streets and made millions in the West into eyewitnesses. The impact of social media on the movements themselves was less clear and often more subtle.[5] That is not to say, however, that social media may not evolve in a different direction. Indeed as communication becomes more ubiquitous, cost drops, and the information space becomes more crowded, the ability of any group to command attention and motivate followers will change.

5. See Jon B. Alterman, "The Revolution Will Not Be Tweeted," *Washington Quarterly* 34, no. 4 (Fall 2011): 103-116.

Where social media has been ineffective has been in translating support into an ability to govern. However broad-based social media campaigns were, they did not equip opposition leaders to bargain effectively with elements of power in their own government. In this way, post-modern politics were not able to triumph over modern politics. This is in the past, however, and we are likely to see new communications tools and new strategies to employ those tools emerge over the next decade. Throughout the Arab uprisings, groups in different countries demonstrated an acute ability to share and learn tactics from each other. Governments demonstrated a similar ability. Innovation is likely to occur in the space, and successes both in promoting change and in reinforcing the status quo are likely to be broadly imitated.

A second and related variable is new ways in which isolated actions have outsized consequences in today's information-rich environment. Videos of the murders of two American journalists in Syria in September 2014 brought the U.S. military to war, even though the videos' production likely involved no more than a handful of people. Similarly, two individuals' attack on the French newspaper *Charlie Hebdo* in January 2015 seized the attention of the world even as it resulted in the death of the attackers. The attacks of September 11, 2001, which involved several dozen people and less than a half-million dollars, completely transformed the security footing of the United States and its allies and precipitated long-running U.S.-led wars in Iraq and Afghanistan. The resources necessary to garner global attention and to bring countries to war are rapidly diminishing. With innovations in technology and storytelling, it is not hard to see how the actions of a dozen could easily affect the fate of tens of millions, time and time again.

A third variable is the price of energy. While oil and gas are not evenly distributed throughout the Middle East, virtually every Middle Eastern economy is tied into the energy economy. Some countries export large quantities of energy, and others export large quantities of labor to countries that export energy. When energy prices are stable and high, the benefits accrue to sitting governments and go into shoring up the status quo. When energy prices are volatile or fall, they force a rethinking of all elements of domestic governance. Most of the major energy exporting states in the Arab world have sufficient accrued reserves to withstand a temporary dip in prices. But just as sustained high prices permitted the implementation of governing strategies predicated on generous benefits for citizens, an end to sustained high prices would force a reevaluation of the strategies. At the same time, less wealthy states have become reliant on support from the Gulf to meet their internal needs, both through direct government support and workers' remittances. Countries such as Jordan, Morocco, and Egypt, which do not have significant reserves on which to draw, are likely to face hard choices sooner.

A fourth variable is geopolitics. Tensions between Iran and Saudi Arabia have many consequences, and among them are increased sectarian tensions in the Arab world. Were there to be a rapprochement between the two states, the effects would ripple throughout the international relations and internal political environments of the region. Perceptions of outsiders' interests in the region, and their commitments to the region, also affect the options available to regional leaders. Governments will make different choices depending on what they see the United States, Russia, China, and Europe committed to doing in the Middle East. The issues affected will include how they treat their neighbors, how they treat their domestic oppositions, and whether they seek to balance against or bandwagon with non-Arab powers such as Israel and Iran.

> *The resources necessary to garner global attention and to bring countries to war are rapidly diminishing.*

The final variable is the outcome of the various political experiments unfolding throughout the Arab world. Governments and publics alike are looking for examples of success, and they are wary of examples of failure. Diminishing security in Yemen, Libya, Iraq, and Syria makes many cautious of change. Cautious democratization in Tunisia, or what may emerge as a moderating authoritarianism in Egypt, will be closely watched experiments throughout the region. At the same time, governments and publics alike will closely watch the efforts of nongovernmental groups to gain influence in governmental decisionmaking and to challenge governments' monopoly on power.

In facing these challenges, governments have an array of traditional tools at their disposal. The first involves the use of elite networks and patronage to create support for government action. Governments have tremendous resources with which they can reward supporters, and the effect of those resources is especially pronounced in the Middle East, where government-centered activities represent a large percentage of the national economy. Government regulatory policy can create or destroy fortunes, and the legal system is often not robust enough to resist efforts that seek to create economic winners based on political loyalty. This is true not only in the oil-rich states of the Gulf, but even in many of the region's republics, where the private sector remains relatively weak, the informal economy is large, and government favor can make or break a business.

Maintaining those elite business networks is a vital task that requires ongoing maintenance. Arguably, both the Ben Ali regime in Tunisia and the Mubarak regime in Egypt erred because they lost the trust of the business elites, as family members' economic activities began to squeeze out powerful economic actors. In Egypt in particular, some argued that the military was losing faith that a government led by Gamal Mubarak would protect the economic interests of the military institutions themselves, and of retired generals. Also in Egypt, the Muslim Brotherhood's business networks created an important base of support for the new government, but their attacks on the business networks of the Mubarak government created a powerful opposition to President Mohammed Morsi's rule.

The hunger for revolutionary change has clearly dimmed. But what is the hunger for evolutionary change?

While attraction is often the preferred strategy for building alliances, a second—coercion—remains a vital tool for Middle Eastern governments. Some of that coercion relies on the instruments of the police state, whose surveillance capabilities have only grown more robust over the last three quarters of a century. Governments retain heavy sway in the courts, and even the threat of a lawsuit that stretches out over years can be an important inhibitor to action. The other component of coercion is influencing the state-sponsored religious institutions to endorse or discredit different trends in society. While these state-sponsored institutions must be careful to maintain some degree of independence, they also must be careful to sufficiently serve the needs of their political patrons, which they do.

The third tool of governments is their soft power. Nationalism remains a powerful force and an attractive idea, and Middle Eastern governments have been especially successful presenting themselves as the manifestation of the national interest. Governments have tremendous power over public discourse through their control of and ownership of media as well as their influence in educational and religious institutions. It is hard to be more nationalistic than a national government playing to patriotism.

Publics looking at their futures must address the question of their goals. Among publics, the hunger for revolutionary change has clearly dimmed. But what is the hunger for evolutionary change? How much risk are publics willing to take, and how many costs are they willing to pay? Do they see a pathway toward a better future? Perhaps most fundamentally, those in favor of change must articulate a way forward that creates space for peaceful actors but does not allow space for radical actors to overwhelm the system. The experience of the last several years, especially in Syria and Libya, is a cautionary tale.

The broader question for the region is the same one it is been struggling with for much of the last half century. How should governments and their citizens balance between their short-term needs and their long-term goals? The popular narrative has always put the Middle East in a state of perpetual crisis, and it is rare to feel the luxury of feeling able to make sacrifices. King Hussein of Jordan, in 1962, wrote a book about his rule as a young man entitled *Uneasy Lies the Head.*[6] It could be the story of any Middle Eastern leader for the last half century.

Middle Eastern politics are continuing to churn, blending promise and menace, dynamism and stagnation. Among publics, politics evoke a sense of possibility and a sense of dread. Despite all of the changes in recent years, leaders seem even more aware of their own mortality. The former presidents club in the Middle East is a small one, and several remain in jail or under house arrest. The club is growing, however, and some hold out the hope that in the coming years it will grow larger still. ■

---

6. Hussein I, *Uneasy Lies the Head: An autobiography of H.M. King Hussein of Jordan* (London: Heinemann, 1962).

2 The Future of Arab State Power

ROGER OWEN

The events set in train by the Arab uprisings of 2011 have seriously weakened state power—in terms of a capacity to govern, to tax, and to protect citizens—in ways that pose a challenge to the whole postcolonial order in the Arab Middle East.

This weakness is the result of several factors: the overthrow of dictatorial regimes; the serious threat posed to other regimes; the ensuing struggles to create new and more stable constitutional orders; heightened political sectarianism; and the emergence (or resurgence) of militant jihadi movements in Syria, Iraq, Libya, and the Sinai Peninsula. All of this is occurring in a region already marked by serious socioeconomic problems such as high levels of unemployment, homelessness, and displaced refugees and menaced by huge ecological problems, including an acute water shortage, creeping desertification, and a lack of local natural resources apart from oil.

The region's future remains uncertain. Nations with once-powerful regimes (Egypt, Syria, and Iraq) have been profoundly shaken. Another, Sudan, has drifted into two civil wars: one between north and south and a second inside the south itself. Yet another, Libya, is on the brink of collapse. Others countries, notably the two monarchies of Morocco and Jordan and the family-ruled states of the Gulf, have survived, but only as a result of experiments with allowing greater popular inputs into decision-making (Qatar, Yemen, Oman, and Saudi Arabia).

Two exceptions seem to prove the rule: Tunisia, which so far has managed a relatively successful transition toward multiparty democracy, and Algeria, whose experience with so much civil war and upheaval seems to have immunized its people to further bloodletting.

And in all cases, the euphoria produced by the sudden toppling of the corrupt dictatorships created an existential feeling of excitement among the protesters.

In what follows, I examine the politico-historical bases of present problems and possible future trajectories by dividing the Arab states into three groups based on features as such the long-term durability of their basic administrative structures, their ability to control their national territory, and their capacity to reach into society to tax and to influence different groups of citizens. These groups are 1) North Africa, including Egypt, 2) the Fertile Crescent, mainly Syria and Iraq, and 3) the Arab Gulf, including Saudi Arabia and Oman.

NORTH AFRICA

State structures in North Africa were well-established but ranged in their capacities from weak but expansive to controlling but hollow. In neither case was this well-understood before the uprisings. In Egypt and Tunisia, the size of the bureaucracy and the ferocity of the security forces helped to disguise the fact that the regime had little power to direct the lives of its citizens, let alone involve them directly in the development of an economy greatly dependent on tourism and foreign assistance. In Libya, in contrast, whatever unity had been created after independence depended almost entirely on the illusion that its leader had his hands on all the major levers of state power. Hence, the spark that produced the first wave of mass uprisings in Tunisia spread quickly to Egypt and later to Libya. It brought down the Zine el-Abidine Ben Ali and Hosni Mubarak regimes, which were followed some months later by the regime of the late Colonel Muammar el-Qaddafi. In all cases, the army proved unable or unwilling to contain these popular movements, while the police were all too easily brushed aside. And in all cases, the euphoria produced by the sudden toppling of the corrupt dictatorships created an existential feeling of excitement among the protesters. It included the sense that there could be no going back, that things could never be the same again.

Attempts to create new political orders focused on drawing up new or amended constitutions. Countries held elections to produce new governments or constitutional assemblies to manage the transition. In these heady circumstances, it was natural for many participants to feel a sense of empowerment that was not easy to translate into the day-to-day practice of politics—drawing up election manifestos, getting voters to the polls, etc. But these practices were necessary to create viable parties distinguished by different ideological platforms targeting particular political constituencies and different reform agendas.

> *In these heady circumstances, it was natural for many participants to feel a sense of empowerment that was not easy to translate into the day-to-day practice of politics—drawing up election manifestos, getting voters to the polls, etc.*

It followed that the first national elections were won by well-established religious movements such as Egypt's Muslim Brotherhood or Tunisia's Ennahda, neither of which suffered the stigma attached to the corrupt old order. But both then experienced great problems in the perhaps impossible process of converting themselves into governing organizations with detailed platforms of economic and social reform that could produce results. That led in Egypt to the overthrow of Muslim Brotherhood government by the army. In Tunisia, it led to the decision by Ennahda's long-time leader, Rached Ghannouchi, to enter a coalition of Tunisian national parties while throwing out almost all of his religious baggage.

In Egypt, neither the extent of the state's grasp nor the particular entanglements between the state and the economy has changed much. For members of Egypt's traditional political class who took part in the system of crony capitalism of the late Mubarak years—in which they managed elections in exchange for access to both wealth and influence—then-General Abdel Fattah al-Sisi's coup undoubtedly came as a relief after the chronic uncertainties of the Muslim Brotherhood's rule. Nevertheless, given the significant role played by the army in the Egyptian economy, it was not immediately clear how those elites would find ways of preserving their business influence. One way is becoming evident: the rules drawn up for the 2015 parliamentary elections reserved three-quarters of the seats for individuals running as independent candidates, a system clearly designed to favor those with money and local connections. Those elections are now indefinitely on hold following a judicial ruling against the electoral law's validity.

Egypt's political future seems likely to be a turbulent one now that Sisi faces increasing international pressure to implement reforms that might lead to inflationary pressure and economic hardship in the short term. What Sisi has been able only to postpone is a difficult choice between holding an over-managed set of elections in 2015 and still further delay. At the same time, he is following the path first established by one of his predecessors, Gamal Abdel Nasser, of trying to consolidate power by getting the economy right first—including by creating new jobs for the many hundreds of thousands of those permanently out of work. As this cycle repeats, there is little sign either of the state growing stronger (in the sense of its capacity) or of its retreating at all from what remain essentially statist economic policies.

Tunisia's passage toward a multiparty democracy was a great deal easier for a number of reasons: its smaller size, its much smaller army, the moderate leadership of its main religious movement (Ennahda), and an electoral system predicated on the need to encourage coalitions and compromise. Still, the process leading from dictatorship to the election, first of a new parliament, then of a new president (the 88-year-old Béji Caïd Essebsi), ended up taking more than a year longer than originally planned. Yet even this might prove to have been a blessing in disguise, with voters seeing Essebsi's long service to a succession of regimes as an historic advantage; he came to represent a kind of wise father figure well-suited to shepherding society into the new era.

Huge problems remain, however. Some are shared with Egypt: desert security, desertification, and problems connected with attracting foreign investment in a shrinking tourist industry. But others are more distinct, such as the fact that some 3,000 young Tunisian jihadists have disappeared to fight in Syria and Iraq since 2011, one of the largest foreign contingents. While political and security concerns dominated the agenda in the first few years following the overthrow of Ben Ali, almost nothing has been done to address these challenges. To date, therefore, there is no apparent recipe for state shrinkage in Tunisia, and no reason, as in Egypt, to suppose anything but a continuation of the existing patterns of cronyism produced wherever the boundaries between business interests and the state remain so porous.

THE ARAB EAST

While North Africa consists of a series of relatively well-established state structures, those to be found in Syria, Lebanon, and Iraq have had a much more checkered history in the postcolonial period. One factor was the relatively short-lived period of colonial rule itself, which gave little time to create the central national institutions needed to govern and maintain order. A second was the existence of substantial religious and racial minorities such as the Kurds, sometimes living in relatively inaccessible and uncontrollable areas, and whose members came to form a significant component of each country's officer corps, such as the Alawis in Syria.

These factors combined with a popular sense of humiliation caused by the failure to destroy the nascent state of Israel in 1948-1949. The result: a series of military coups that destroyed the old landed ruling class. The leaders of these coups created larger and stronger state structures designed to control their restive populations and to introduce the type of educational and welfare arrangements characteristic of revolutionary Egypt. The result for both Iraq and Syria was a long period of authoritarian rule under the Assad family in Syria and Saddam Hussein in Iraq. Both regimes combined the stick of merciless repression—Kanan Makiya's "Republic of Fear"—and the carrot of social welfare to maintain their rule, until neither regime could afford its growing costs and each was forced to seek alternative forms of revenue. Syria began to open to private capital, while Iraq tried to take over oil-rich Kuwait in 1990 and then, when this was thwarted by international intervention, to sell its oil at heavily discounted prices during the sanctions regime that followed.

The leaders of these coups created larger and stronger state structures designed to control their restive populations and to introduce the type of educational and welfare arrangements characteristic of revolutionary Egypt.

One unhappy situation was then followed by another. In Iraq, the U.S. invasion and occupation in 2003 almost entirely dismantled the old state structures—the presidency, the ruling Ba'ath Party, the internal security apparatus, and the army. In their place was a puppet regime, assisted by U.S. and British advisers, that presided over a rag-bag of ministries with little control outside the major cities of Mosul, Baghdad, and Basra. Even worse was to come. Prime Minister Nouri al-Maliki, who first came to power in 2006, proceeded to use his considerable powers of patronage and intrigue to create a set of domestic fiefs, including a military whose higher-command simply crumbled away at the first concerted attack by the highly motivated jihadi fighters of Islamic State group (ISG) in 2014.

In Syria, state structures were not dismantled in the same way, but the geographical area the Syrian state controls has eroded. Given the porous nature of its borders, a combination of local rebel forces and foreign jihadists has severely limited the Assad regime's control over large swaths of the countryside beyond the cities of Damascus and Aleppo. As had been proved over and over again in the colonial period, whether in Syria itself or elsewhere, airpower was insufficient to police a restive population in lands awash with weapons in the hands of disaffected young men.

> *Oil, as it turned out, was something of a two-edged sword.*

THE ARAB GULF

The notion of the "state" means something different and unusual when applied to family-ruled entities in the Arab Gulf, including Saudi Arabia and Oman. For one thing, these states have historically relied on others (first the United Kingdom, and then the United States) to protect them from external and, occasionally, internal assault. This was true both in the days before oil was discovered in the 1930s and later, when the Gulf states' new wealth was eyed with great envy by larger neighbors such as Iraq, Syria, and Egypt. For another, they have historically depended heavily on foreigners to staff most of their domestic ministries even though, in each case, the man nominally in charge was drawn either from the ruling family or from a small band of foreign-educated technocrats such as the onetime Saudi Minister of Oil, Shaykh Zaki Yamani.

Oil, as it turned out, was something of a two-edged sword. It provided great riches to the ruling families themselves. But once they decided to create a cradle-to-grave welfare state for those citizens they deemed truly national, maintaining their economies and welfare states required an increasing foreign labor force. First came Arabic speakers drawn largely from Egypt, Lebanon, and Jordan, and later men from the Indian subcontinent and women from Indonesia, Thailand, and other parts of Southeast Asia. To make matters even more complicated, attempts to prevent the buildup of a huge permanent population of non-nationals soon foundered on the fact that, having surrendered control over these same migrant laborers to their native employers, the latter were unwilling to ensure that their employees actually returned home after the time period stipulated in their contracts had passed. Other regulations designed to prevent migrant laborers staying on, such as bans on their owning property, opening their own businesses, or bringing in their wives and families to join them, were also openly flouted. All that then remained of each state's ability to control who passed in and out across its borders was a well-managed security arm, developed in the first instance to protect the ruling family, but employed more and more at airports and other points of entry and exit to monitor particular lists of persons regarded as unusually dangerous. That may be starting to change, as first Saudi Arabia and now Kuwait have embarked on aggressive deportation campaigns.

What does this leave of the traditional instruments of state power as defined by Max Weber and other writers? Certainly these countries demonstrate a version of sovereignty, enshrined in their membership, jointly or severally, of the United Nations and various other international institutions and protected on occasions by joint international action, as in the case of international efforts to repel Iraq's occupation of Kuwait in 1990. These countries also possess the trappings of what Sami Zubaida has called the "Jacobin model" of the modern state: flags, capital cities, a single political field, and a particular set of legal and educational institutions. Finally, of course, there are the "national narratives" beginning with the arrival of members of the present ruling families in Kuwait or Bahrain or Abu Dhabi or Dubai or elsewhere. Nevertheless, several of them lack other features of modern state power, including a monopoly on policing and violence—shared with their own citizens—or a de jure legitimacy respected by all the permanent residents living within their national boundaries. Nor does it seem likely that these lacunae will be addressed in the near future. Rather the reverse is more likely. One of the basic factors essential to the Gulf states' success so far seems to have been the secrecy with which they are governed and the almost complete lack of accountability of their ruling families. But this hardly breeds respect or legitimacy.

WHITHER THE ARAB STATE?

Two conclusions can be put forward with a reasonable degree of confidence. One is that we are unlikely to see any shrinkage of the state itself in size, in the ferocity of its security forces, or in the central role played in the management of the lives of most Arab populations. The exceptions are Tunisia and those unfortunate countries in which state capacity to repress has been undermined by foreign invasion or civil war.

Second, most Arab regimes will engage in new ways of managing their societies, although, in most instances, they will stop a long way short of the type of democratic participation characteristic of the majority of their European neighbors. One can imagine developments along two separate axes. The first, already mentioned in the case of Egypt and the oil statelets of the Gulf, is that states will increasingly seek to involve their citizens in the creation of profitable partnerships or major development initiatives to give them a sense that they have a stake in the future of their states, which will nonetheless remain centrally controlled. An example of this is the Suez Canal Investment Project. According to a Baseera poll, members of 2.2 million households have bought

Suez Canal Investment certificates, nearly two-thirds of them using either bank deposits or previously untapped savings.[1] Sisi has asked Egyptians to get personally invested, and many have responded.

A second likely development is that governments will make use of recent advances in technology, especially surveillance technology. This may include basic acts like phone-tapping, but could also extend to better monitoring of populations by creating fixed addresses for every house and family—something previously possible only in Egypt, which conducted regular national censuses. This is not to say that better mapping and data of populations need be an entirely police or security affair. Policy initiatives in Europe and North America, for example, have demonstrated how such data can enable ministries of education and social welfare to target disadvantaged groups with subsidized food and medicine or create opportunities for their children to partake of distance or after-hours education.

Sisi has asked Egyptians to get personally invested, and many have responded.

A final possibility is that governments might use the power of the state to provide the infrastructure that would underpin a vibrant civil society. A move in this direction would begin with a shift toward legal structures permitting the type of private associations that have become such a critical part of the Tunisian social scene. Some are engaged in monitoring government and parliamentary activity, while some are experimenting with new ways of forming pressure groups to lobby for various types of social reform.

Whether such measures will end up creating more or less viable state structures with full control over their boundaries must still be a matter of concern, the more so as jihadi groups inside and just beyond their borders threaten both regime authority and social cohesion. In some cases, notably Iraq, Syria, and Yemen, the immediate future appears to be a return to something like the old Ottoman order, where administrative power was concentrated in a series of provincial capitals: Damascus, Aleppo, Mosul, Baghdad, Basra, Sana'a, and Aden. None was able either to achieve a stable preponderance over the others or over the countryside between. In others, notably North Africa, the scenario looking ahead is quite different. The desert borders are fragile. Jihadists, smugglers, and others can move easily east-west and north-south through the Sahara. This will mean, at the very least, an attenuation of their post-independence sovereignty and a decreasing ability to govern and provide security. That might lead to pressure to create supranational Arab security agencies charged with doing what each government cannot do on its own. ■

1. Magued Osman, "Press Release: The poll conducted by the Egyptian Center for Public Opinion Research (Baseera) on Egyptians' participation in funding the New Suez Canal Project," Baseera, 2014, http://www.baseera.com.eg/pdf_poll_file_en/Suez%20Canal%20certificates-En.pdf.

3 The Great Powers in the New Middle East

JOHN MCLAUGHLIN

Trying to nail down how the world's major powers—the United States, China, Russia, and Europe—see and set strategy for the Middle East these days has never been more challenging. Power relationships globally are in flux. The Middle East is in turmoil. And the powers themselves are struggling through difficult transitions. The metaphors commonly used to describe today's international web of crises—three-dimensional chess, Rubik's cube—fall short of capturing the sheer complexity of it all, especially when it comes to the Middle East. A more apt metaphor might be the sensation of walking into the middle of a barroom brawl: it's hard to be sure who started it, who is allied with whom, exactly what is at issue, who just changed sides, who is fighting, who is just observing, where your leverage is, and how to break it up.

THE STRATEGIC CONTEXT

The contemporary context of the Middle East determines a great deal. Major powers have to formulate their Middle East strategies today in a different strategic context from either the Cold War or what came after.[1] During the Cold War, direct great power competition in the region was not as intense or head-on as in Europe or East Asia. The former was the center of NATO-Warsaw Pact confrontation, and the latter the arena for war, either directly or by proxy, in countries such as Korea and Vietnam. But Russia, China, the

1. Henry Kissinger, "On the Assembly of a New World Order," *Wall Street Journal*, August 29, 2014. Kissinger's latest thinking captures the fluid nature of the international system at this stage.

United States, and many European nations nonetheless saw the Middle East in the zero-sum terms so characteristic of the era. This dynamic played out in relations with Egypt and Libya under Gamal Abdel Nasser and Muammar el-Qaddafi, in weapons sales, and in the Arab-Israeli conflicts.

Then the Cold War ended with the fall of the Berlin Wall and the collapse of the Soviet Union between 1989 and 1991. The international system entered a period during which the major powers' approaches to the Middle East became more fluid, either by necessity or choice.

During the early post-Cold War years, Russia and China were mindful of the Middle East but thoroughly absorbed with internal transformations. Russia moved from a command economy to private enterprise. China was digesting Deng Xiaoping's market economic reforms and purging sympathizers of the 1989 Tiananmen Square protests. Without the overlay of U.S.-Soviet rivalry, Europe focused on rebuilding traditional relationships in the Middle East, deepening integration within the European Union, and laying the groundwork for bringing in former Soviet satellite countries as new members.

Meanwhile, the United States gained as free a hand as it will ever have in international affairs as the only surviving and prosperous superpower. It was absorbed in consolidating its post-Cold War position in Europe (the uniting of Germany within NATO, for example), building a new relationship with Russia, and dealing with problems in the Balkans. As for the Middle East, the United States' main concerns were terrorism, the flow of oil, the Israeli-Palestinian dispute, and two wars in Iraq.[2]

With the Cold War over, Middle Eastern competition among the great powers was separated for the first time in decades from a global struggle. The great powers began to see their relations with the region once again more in terms of individual national interests, pursued mainly in bilateral relations with Middle Eastern nations.

With the Cold War over, Middle Eastern competition among the great powers was separated for the first time in decades from a global struggle.

The next stage of great power relations kicked in with the global financial crisis of 2008, which weakened confidence in the United States. At the same time, Russia became more assertive, as evidenced by its occupation of parts of Georgia. And the perception grew that China was "rising" in a way bound to challenge U.S. international dominance.

2. John McLaughlin, "Navigating Threats in the Dark," *Global Brief,* October 14, 2014, http://globalbrief.ca/blog/2013/11/11/navigating-threats-in-the-strategic-dark/. This interview was intended to sketch out some of the challenges likely to face the United States in an era when it is likely to be less dominant.

So if there is a moment when we can say the United States' "Superpower Moment" began to pass, it is probably 2008. This also is the moment when major powers maneuvering in the Middle East and elsewhere were thrust into a world akin to the age of balance-of-power politics, which dominated diplomacy in earlier times. In that context, the United States is still the world's most powerful nation in the sense that few problems can be managed without it. Yet there are few problems the United States can manage alone or lead the response to without challenge.[3]

As the major powers were adjusting to these new dynamics, the Middle East was rocked by three phenomena that changed the character of the region and the terms on which outsiders must engage it. *First,* the Iraq war polarized the countries of the region and roiled relations among the major outside powers. *Second,* Islamic extremism sunk deeper roots and sparked divisions among outside powers about how to respond to it. And *third,* the region experienced the so-called Arab Spring, which upset not only the domestic norms of many countries but also changed many of the personalities and institutions that served for years as conduits to the outside powers.

It is against this complex strategic backdrop and history that the major powers must now formulate their policies toward the Middle East. It is not surprising therefore that those policies are marked by contradictions, frequent swerves, and internal tensions.

RUSSIA

In the Putin era, Russia must fit the Middle East into a strategy with three principal goals:

- To consolidate a Russian sphere of influence in the "near abroad"—neighboring countries such as Ukraine that were part of the Soviet Union
- To tighten domestic political and economic control
- To restore Russian influence in critical regions such as the Middle East, where Moscow wants to fight terrorist threats, has important economic and political interests, and sees itself in competition with the United States and its partners[4]

Not all of Moscow's interests and pursuits in the Middle East are destined to be at odds with Washington's. Russia shares with the United States a keen sense of the threats that can come from Islamic extremists. Throughout his career, Putin

3. John McLaughlin, "What's Happening to American Power," *Ozy,* July 17, 2014, http://www.ozy.com/#!/c-notes/the-spy-who-told-me-the-end-of-the-pax-americana/32760.article.
4. Roland Dannreuther, "Russia and the Middle East: A Cold War Paradigm," *Europe-Asia Studies* 64, no. 3 (May 2012): 543–560. Dannreuther does an excellent job contrasting Russia's Cold War approach with today's and laying out the main lines of Russian policy.

has presented himself as an opponent of Islamic extremism, mostly when it helped foment independence movements in the partly Muslim Russian Caucasus such as the Chechen Republic. During the two Chechen wars in 1994 and 1999, jihadi fighters migrated to Russia from the Middle East and South Asia, especially via the Pankisi Gorge in Georgia. With Middle Eastern donors fueling nascent Islamic movements in Tatarstan and Central Asia, Russia will monitor Islamic movements in the Middle East and seek ways to combat them.

In some of its regional relations, competing goals force Russia to walk a fine line. Nothing highlights the delicacy, difficulty, and complexity of Russian diplomacy more than its relations with Iran. Since the Iranian Revolution in 1979, Moscow has been wary of Iranian influence on its southern periphery, especially in nominally Muslim Central Asian states such as Azerbaijan, Tajikistan, and Turkmenistan. Yet Russia helped Iran realize some aspects of its nuclear program such as construction of the nuclear reactor at Bushehr. At the same time, Moscow has stopped short of endorsing Iran's acquisition of nuclear weapons and joined the West in endorsing sanctions against Tehran. But Russia always pushed for a less stringent package than the United States wanted.

Russia also has sought to move beyond the Soviet-era dependence on ideological ties and weapons sales by developing a web of commercial relations with states in the region. For example, although NATO member Turkey has been a Russian strategic rival historically, it has become Russia's largest trading partner in the region. Trade increased from about $4 billion annually in the 1990s to around $30 billion over the last decade. More than 60 percent of Ankara's natural gas imports come from Russia. Turkey is followed by Iran and Egypt in the volume of Russian trade.

When it comes to weapons sales, Russia has customers ranging from Syria to Egypt, Iran, and Libya. Its largest client in the region is Algeria, which purchases more than 90 percent of its weaponry from Russia (11 percent of Russia's total arms exports). Algeria is the most autocratic of the region's regimes and has yet to experience the turbulence its immediate neighbors did during the Arab Spring.[5]

Russia's broader geopolitical motives in the Middle East center on its determination to be a player on the main regional issues that engage the rest of the world. In pursuit of that goal, it has worked to broaden its web of cooperative relations to include states such as Israel and formerly hostile nations such as Saudi Arabia. Meanwhile, Moscow's financial and weapons support and its historical ties to Syria give it crucial leverage in any resolution of the Syrian conflict. Similarly, it holds strong cards in the current P5+1

5. Siemon T. Wezeman and Peter Wezeman, "Trends in International Arms Transfers, 2013," Stockholm International Peace Research Institute (SIPRI), March 2014, http://books.sipri.org/files/FS/SIPRIFS1403.pdf.

The West cannot reach an agreement with Tehran absent Moscow's acquiescence.

negotiations with Iran on reducing or dismantling its nuclear program. The West cannot reach an agreement with Tehran absent Moscow's acquiescence.

In sum, Russia recognizes the importance of all the changes underway in the Middle East and is building on traditional alliance relationships to assure its leverage in any resolution of regional issues.

CHINA

For a long time, the formula many relied on to understand Chinese policy toward the Middle East was: energy security = economic development = political stability. China's policy toward the region was all about oil and commerce, with little engagement in regional politics. Energy—55 percent of China's comes from the Middle East—fueled for years the double-digit economic growth of China's export-driven economy. That provided jobs and rising prosperity for millions coming onto the job market every year. This in turn bought political calm in a system that otherwise might have had trouble continuing to justify stern, one-party rule.

The formula is still at the heart of China's approach to the region, but Beijing now has concerns about all three elements of it. Like all things touching the Middle East these days, it's not quite that simple any more.[6]

Energy security remains an abiding concern for Beijing. But both the turmoil in the Middle East and worry about the U.S. role in the region have heightened that concern. Beijing frets that it may not be able to rely on Washington to provide security in the Middle East as a kind of "public good" for the rest of the world. The latter concern stems from U.S. defense budget cuts and the now widely anticipated U.S. move to energy self-sufficiency in the next couple of decades. While there are still many uncertainties, rising U.S. energy production, largely from extraction of shale gas and oil, combined with declining demand, appears likely to diminish U.S. reliance on supplies from the Middle East and elsewhere.

---

6. Richard L. Russell, "America Turns East, China Turns West," *National Interest*, February 28, 2014; David Schenker, "China's Middle East Footprint," *Los Angeles Times*, April 26, 2013; Christina Lin, "China's Strategic Shift Toward the Region of the Four Seas," Institute for Strategic, Political, Security and Economic Consultancy (ISPSW), no. 226, April 2013. Lin provides an excellent overview of China's thinking and much of the data in this section is drawn from her work. Russell adds the contrast between U.S. and Chinese approaches. Schenker spells out some of China's worries about its vulnerabilities at this time.

Beijing probably takes some comfort from knowing that Washington's close European and Asian allies—particularly Japan and Korea—rely heavily on Middle Eastern supplies. American fidelity to alliance relationships will keep the United States reliably on the job in the Persian Gulf and elsewhere. Still, Beijing cannot rely exclusively on the U.S. Navy and fears that in the event of rising tensions with Washington, the United States could block the Malacca Straits, through which pass about 80 percent of China's energy imports. Disputes could arise over a number of issues, from Taiwan to East China Sea disputes with U.S. ally Japan.

China is not standing apart to the degree it has in the past.

Such concerns are behind China's aggressive push for naval modernization in recent years and its expansion into port facilities—the so-called "String of Pearls"—from the Chinese mainland along Indian Ocean ports and into the Middle East. These are largely commercial arrangements for port access and refueling. All of this comes under the heading of what Chinese naval commanders refer to as a shift from coastal defense to "far sea defense." Accompanying the shift has been an increased emphasis on showing the flag in the area of Suez and the Mediterranean—an outreach prompted by concern about energy security. To supplement the maritime presence, China is building a rail and pipeline network linking part of the Middle East to China via Central Asia.[7]

Strains appearing in the Chinese economic model make ensuring energy supplies a top priority for the Chinese leadership. Rising prosperity has pushed up wages, which makes Chinese exports less competitive. Growth has dipped into the 7 percent range and the country remains burdened by large state enterprises that soak up 35 percent of economic activity. So new Chinese leader Xi Jinping has embarked on an aggressive campaign to stamp out corruption and move economic decisionmaking into a more commercial versus political mode. Given all the uncertainties he is dealing with, one thing Xi Jinping cannot risk is access to energy.

This sense of urgency has not yet moved Beijing to strive for major player status in the Middle East's many disputes. But China is not standing apart to the degree it has in the past. It contributes to peacekeeping forces in Lebanon. It makes naval port calls in the Gulf. And it is striving for closer relations with a series of regional powers ranging from Turkey to Egypt.

---

7. Süreyya Yiğit, "Russian and Chinese Influences in the Middle East and Eurasia," *OrtadoguAnaliz 5*, no. 59 (November 2013): 76–85, http://www.orsam.org.tr/en/enUploads/Article/Files/2013124_makale8.pdf

Meanwhile, it must worry about the extremism it sees in the Middle East encouraging the restive population of Xinjiang Province in Western China, whose ethnic Uyghurs, a Turkic people, have shown up amid Islamic fighters in locales such as Afghanistan. The Uyghurs are ethnic cousins of Turkey's Uyghurs, making improved relations with Turkey, which has sometimes criticized Chinese policy toward Xinjiang, all the more important in Beijing's calculus.

A core principle of Chinese foreign policy is to oppose regime change, at least when managed by Western powers, fearing that they have the same goal for China. So the Arab Spring and its aftermath in various countries was unsettling for Beijing. It not only disrupted carefully cultivated commercial relations with regimes undergoing change; it has also drawn Beijing more into the region's politics. Beijing's anti-regime change policy meant it was frustrated when its abstention on the United Nations resolution endorsing intervention in Libya led to coalition action that went beyond humanitarian relief to regime change. Beijing will veto similar resolutions on Syria.

Beijing's fear of regime change is exacerbated by China's historic sense of "encirclement." Washington's "rebalance" toward Asia and its renewed activism in the Middle East serve to heighten Beijing's concerns. All of this points to a more activist Chinese posture in the Middle East in the future, centering not just on commercial relations but increasingly on political and military ties.

EUROPE AND THE UNITED STATES

Europe and the United States have been more deeply involved in the Middle East than other major powers. The United States has been drawn to the region because of its perceived global responsibilities, commitment to Israel's security, and energy needs. Europe is pulled in by many factors, some shared with the United States, some unique—simple proximity, colonial history, energy dependence, and two world wars fought partly on Middle Eastern battlefields.[8]

By any standard, these are unique times in European and U.S. engagement with the region. On the one hand, the interests of Europe and the United States in the Middle East largely converge. And they have a generally shared conception of the direction in which they would like to see the region evolve politically and economically—toward democratic norms, more equalitarian societies, and open market economies. In this regard, they differ sharply from China, firmly committed to one-party rule, and Russia, which is trending in that direction.

---

8. Kristin Archick and Derek E. Mix, "The United States and Europe: Responding to Change in the Middle East and North Africa," Congressional Research Service, June 12, 2013, http://fas.org/sgp/crs/row/R43105.pdf. This is a very good overview with the emphasis on Europe's economic engagement with a Middle East in transition.

Yet, despite this common outlook by the United States and Europe and the great power they could potentially wield together, they have seldom had less leverage in the region. This stems from a variety of factors.

First, with so many of the countries in transition, many of the personalities and institutions with which links had been formed are gone. And while both the United States and Europe have been highly influential in the democratic evolutions in Eastern Europe, neither encounters in the Middle East anything approaching the strong desire for alliance and societal imitation that the East Europeans had. Middle Eastern countries in transition are interested mainly in economic and military assistance. This comes at a time when both the United States and Europe are struggling fitfully through slow economic recoveries and are unable to provide what these nations want.

Despite this common outlook by the United States and Europe and the great power they could potentially wield together, they have seldom had less leverage in the region.

Second, engaging the region now is made more difficult by its very unsettled nature—the sense that politics has yet to crystallize into any predictable pattern that offers a reliable planning horizon for outsiders. Egypt is a case in point. It is common among Middle East watchers to say: as Egypt goes, so goes the Middle East. And yet Egypt has since 2011 been through two major and largely unpredictable transitions—first from Hosni Mubarak's autocratic style to short-lived divisive rule under the Muslim Brotherhood's Mohammed Morsi, then returning to strong central control under the regime of Abdel Fattah al-Sisi. Although Sisi seems firmly in charge, it is hard to be confident that even this regime will endure, given the societal and economic problems he is struggling with and the public's recognition that "the street" has power to turn out rulers.

Third, the level of violence in the Middle East, unprecedented in its pervasiveness in modern times, impedes coherent and consistent policy. This stems from the war in Syria and more recently from the expansion of its most powerful Islamic extremist group, the Islamic State, into Iraq. As this is written, the Islamic State group (ISG) controls a swath of territory stretching from Aleppo in Syria to the outskirts of Baghdad, territory on which it has proclaimed a "caliphate." The United States and Europe agree that the ISG must be rolled back and defeated and that this could take years.

The perceived dangers that come from the war in Syria and Iraq and what amounts to the erasing of the border between the two have pushed aside all but the most essential forms of non-conflict-related engagement. For Europe, the ISG has to be a riveting concern, largely because the EU estimates there are approximately 3,000 Europeans among the roughly 20,000 foreigners who have merged into the ISG's fighters, which rough estimates now put in the range of 30,000 or more. This means that European leaders, more than at any time in the past, must prepare for the possibility of Islamic extremists holding European passports filtering back into their countries. Washington, already troubled by reports of more than 100 Americans among the fighters, shares this concern. Making matters worse for Washington, European passport holders have visa-free passage into the United States.[9]

Finally, while U.S. influence in the Middle East is hard to confidently measure and while Washington has struggled with difficult choices, it appears to have lost much of its clout. Most commonly cited causes are inconsistent responses to political changes, especially in Egypt; backing away from "red lines" promising military action if Syria used chemical weapons; and Saudi and Israeli displeasure over U.S.-led negotiations with Iran intended to render its nuclear program incapable of producing weapons.

Yet the United States burnished its credentials recently by organizing a coalition of disparate regional players and United States allies from elsewhere to fight the ISG. If this remains effective, it will go far to reestablish U.S. leadership in the region. This is of course a huge if, given the uncertainties when forces engage on the battlefield, particularly this unique one.

In sum, there are only a few points of convergence among great power policies toward the Middle East at this tumultuous time. They all want to see terrorism defeated and none of them is comfortable with Iran developing nuclear weapons. But the way to achieve these goals is in dispute, especially between the Western powers and the others. Both China and Russia will balk at any arrangements that involve separatism or require regime change.

The Middle East is now the world's principal laboratory for practicing the new balance-of-power politics likely to characterize the coming decades. It is the arena where the first rounds of a new "Great Game" are playing out. The game has begun, whether the great powers are ready or not. ■

---

9. John McLaughlin, "The Islamic State: The Beast Keeps Growing," *Ozy,* February 23, 2015, http://www.ozy.com/pov/the-islamic-state-the-beast-keeps-growing/39753.

4 The Recurring Rise and Fall of Political Islam

PAUL SALEM

For political Islamic groups, the past four years have been the best of years and the worst of years. In this period, the Arab world's oldest and largest political Islamic movement, the Muslim Brotherhood (MB), had its biggest ever victory in its homeland of Egypt, followed a year later by its biggest defeat. In the same period, a jihadi-salafi group, the Islamic State group (ISG), conquered large swaths of these two countries and announced the establishment of the Islamic State and the restoration of the caliphate in the person of its leader, Abu Bakr al-Baghdadi.[1] This hyper-radical jihadi proto-state attracted an international fringe of radical fighters. But it caused a revulsion among majorities throughout the Arab world and triggered the establishment of an international and regional military coalition against it. Other non-jihadi salafi groups formed political parties and joined the political process after the Arab uprisings and are trying to navigate the troubled waters between the MB and the jihadi radicals.

Some states have accommodated MB and salafi-affiliated Islamist political parties while others have moved to banish them. New regional and international alliances have sprung up for and against the MB. All states in the region have moved to fight the radical jihadists, while the extremists

1. The Islamic State group (ISG) is also known by several names, including ISIS (the Islamic State of Iraq and al Sham), ISIL (the Islamic State of Iraq and the Levant), and IS.

have succeeded in occupying spaces left open by failing states.

Majorities that voted Islamist parties to power in Egypt and Tunisia turned into majorities that protested their monopolization of power and attempts to Islamize the state and society. In 2012, it appeared as if MB-led political Islam would define the future of the Middle East. By the end of 2013, the MB had suffered a strong blow in Egypt and had to step down from power in Tunisia. By 2014, it was radical jihadism that had once more reclaimed center stage. Political Islam thus has been an integral part of the turbulent dynamics of the past four years and is likely to be a complex and dynamic factor in the region's politics for many years to come.

The Islamist parties had their own weakness: while they could win elections, they were unprepared to govern.

Interestingly, Islamic movements were not an early part of the sudden and massive uprisings of the winter of 2011. In most countries, MB and salafi groups had been in uneasy accommodations with authoritarian regimes. State elites monopolized political and economic power and closed down political space while allowing Islamist groups to occupy social and cultural space. The uprisings were originally spearheaded by youth who were not part of the old bargains. Joining them was a population fed up with the long-standing status quo and eager for change. Islamist parties joined in once they saw the train leaving the station. The uprisings did not have an Islamist message, but rather clamored inarticulately for some form of social democracy: an end to dictatorship and repression, the establishment of elected and accountable government, and the provision of freedom, dignity, bread, jobs, and social justice.

While these slogans dominated the uprisings, it was the Islamist parties that won the post-uprising elections. It is not because they commanded natural majorities, but because they had the grassroots networks and party organizations that could run and win election campaigns. Meanwhile, the youth, liberals, nationalists, leftists, and other groups remained divided. They were good at organizing protests and appearing on talk shows, but not at grassroots party organizing. Indeed, had the non-Islamist anti-regime factions backed one candidate in the Egyptian presidential elections of 2012, their candidate would have won the presidency, and Egypt would have embarked on a different path in its troubled transition.

The Islamist parties had their own weakness: while they could win elections, they were unprepared to govern. This should not be surprising, as few of them imagined in 2010 that they would be anywhere near power in 2012. Their biggest failing was perhaps political, not technocratic. They mistook their narrow electoral victories as a broad endorsement of their Islamist agenda. In fact it was the reluctant nod of a public eager for change and looking for a party to lead an inclusive transition. Indeed, the Islamists' one year of power in Egypt and Tunisia was a botched opportunity in more ways than one. They not only alienated electoral allies and antagonized powerful state institutions, but they also upset broad cross sections of the population. Many citizens had come to view them sympathetically as long-persecuted opposition groups and hoped that they would bring more abilities and probity to government. They were disappointed to find that once in government, the Islamists exhibited many of the same failings and ineptitudes of past politicians.

Not surprisingly, secularists bristled at the Islamists' attempts to push Islamic law. Many observant Muslims also bristled at the idea that their government and politicians were now going to tell them how to pray and practice their own religion. In the case of Egypt, in particular, rarely has a party lost so much by winning so handily.

The MB in Egypt is at a low point in its long history. It is not the first time it has been persecuted by the state. But the campaign is deeper than previous ones, and it was accompanied—especially early on—by a broad public outcry against the group. The accommodation with the state that it enjoyed under Anwar al-Sadat and Hosni Mubarak is gone. And the bridges and sympathies that the MB had built with other groups and sectors of society are also in tatters. The MB is and will remain a major group within society. But while it had maneuvered to the center of the revolution and rose to power, it is now on the edges of both power and the social center, fighting to get back in. And perhaps that word, fighting, is the key to guessing at its future.

In interpreting this demise, the MB has chosen to focus on the military coup of July 3 rather than the public uprising of June 30. It focuses on the illegalities of removing an elected president by force and the violent crackdowns that ensued. It largely ignores the tenuous illegitimacy of clinging to power after the majority of the public, in the midst of a historic revolution, was demanding an end to MB rule and the holding of fresh presidential elections.

Few Islamists have attempted such a self-critique. Their preoccupation with their removal by the military led many to conclude that the democratic path to power is rigged against them and that they have to fight force with force. For the time being, there seems no path toward reintegration. The MB is still maximalist in its position of restoring the Mohammed Morsi presidency. But the government of President Abdel Fattah al-Sisi has declared the MB a terrorist organization and seeks no accommodation.

Meanwhile the main salafi party, Nour, is trying to occupy some of the Islamist political space the MB vacated. The Nour Party had fallen out with the MB during the latter's year in power and sided with the 2013 popular uprising and military intervention. The next parliamentary elections, originally set for March but then postponed, will determine Nour's political strength moving forward. Although the party promotes an Islamist political discourse that President Sisi generally rails against, the party has made clear that it is his political ally. Indeed, Nour might seek to recreate the old relationship between the Mubarak regime and the MB, in which the latter enjoyed a wide presence socially—and occasionally politically—as long as it did not directly challenge the ruling authority.

Although the MB's saga in Egypt is indeed central, given the size and history of the movement there, the movement has affiliates throughout the Arab world. Indeed, around 2012 it appeared that an MB network was poised to dominate the next decade or more of Arab political life. It had notched victories in the bellwether Arab spring countries of Tunisia and Egypt, had a strong presence in Yemen, Libya, Morocco, and Syria, and won strong backing from Turkey and Qatar. But the debacle in Egypt, the stalemate in Tunisia, and other developments, including a strong backlash from powerful Gulf Cooperation Council (GCC) countries, blocked that dominance.

For his part, President Sisi has been well aware of the political pull of religion. The Grand Imam of al-Azhar and the Coptic Pope stood alongside him when he announced the removal of Morsi. And in a New Year's speech before Azhar, he called on the institution to lead a revolution in Islamic thinking. He charged that contemporary Islamic trends were "antagonizing the entire world." He called on Azhar and other established institutions to lead a reform of religious teaching and communication to "suit the modern age." But it is doubtful whether old religious institutions such as Azhar can successfully reinvigorate themselves to compete with more dynamic political movements that have strong grassroots networks and social media skills.

In Tunisia, polarization between the Islamist ruling Ennahda party and wide cross sections of the political and civil society opposition had reached extremes in 2013. The assassination of two prominent anti-government leaders was pushing the country toward possible civil conflict, and attempts to reach a compromise solution were getting nowhere. But Ennahda was sticking to its positions, leaning on its electoral mandate and confident that with rising MB power in Egypt and elsewhere, they were on the winning side of history.

The events in Egypt in the summer of 2013 reshuffled the political deck in Tunisia. The opposition redoubled its efforts to bring down the government, but here Ennahda chose accommodation over confrontation. The party agreed to step down from power, accept a neutral interim government, and engage in fresh talks to draft a constitution. Realizing that the Islamist agenda was the party's and not a point of national consensus, Ennahda dropped its insistence on Islamist clauses in the new constitution. The draft that was unanimously approved is remarkably secular, civic, and democratic.

> *The events in Egypt in the summer of 2013 reshuffled the political deck in Tunisia.*

Ennahda had the luxury of learning from the Egyptian MB's missteps, the good fortune of not facing a formidable military establishment, and a wise leadership that could differentiate between party platforms and the exigencies of pluralistic national constitution-building and politics. Ennahda in Tunisia has managed to ride out the turbulence and will be a key player in Tunisia's political life, among other players, for the foreseeable future.

Morocco exhibits a different example of an Islamist party in politics. The king sought to get ahead of the wave of demands unleashed in 2011. He pushed through the passage of a new constitution and invited the MB-affiliated party there, the Party of Justice and Development (PJD), to form the government after it did well in parliamentary elections. That accommodation between the monarchy and the PJD-led government has endured.

Of course the Moroccan case is special in a number of ways. First, it is a monarchy, not a republic, and hence the king can afford to open up electoral space without putting his ultimate rule in electoral question. Second, he has strong Islamist legitimacy and authority himself as heir to the Alaouite dynasty, which claims descent from the prophet and grants the king the title of "commander of the faithful." Third, the king retains extensive powers in the state and over key ministries in the government. Fourth, the PJD openly models itself on the Turkish Justice and Development Party (AKP) and seeks to be a mainstream political party with a conservative base, rather than a strictly Islamist party pushing an Islamist agenda. Nevertheless, the Moroccan case demonstrates that systemic conditions can affect political Islamic parties and that under the right conditions and with the right leadership, Islamist parties and leaders with MB roots can be encouraged to move toward the political center.

The MB-affiliated party in Yemen, Islah, also remains a significant political player. It has its own peculiar social and political history. It was founded in 1990 with support from the Ali Abdullah Saleh government as a counterbalance to the Socialist Party. It was based on a strong tribal backbone but also held together MB-leaning groups in the urban centers and more salafi sheikhs from the regions. The tribal "Sheikh of Sheikhs," Abdullah al-Ahmar, led the party until his death in 2007. After that, it drifted into the opposition and became part of the uprising of 2011.

Islah was a key player in the transition and national dialogue process but has lost ground over the past year. It was on bad terms with former President Saleh and developed bad relations with President Abd Rabbuh Mansur Hadi. It lost favor with Saudi Arabia for opposing the sacking of Morsi in Egypt. And it has lost key ground to the Zaydi Shi'ite Houthi movement, which took over the capital in the summer of 2014. The party has also lost some ideological ground to jihadi-salafi groups, most notably al Qaeda, which presents itself as a powerful counterforce to the Houthi movement, and to non-jihadi salafi parties such as the Peace and Development Party. The Islah Party remains an active player in the politics of post-uprising Yemen. But more vibrant political Islamic movements—the Houthi rebellion in the north and al Qaeda—threaten to tear the country apart along sectarian lines.

In Jordan and Kuwait, the MB-affiliated groups—the Islamic Action Front in Jordan and the Islamic Constitutional Movement (or Hadas) in Kuwait—have seen their influence rise and fall largely echoing the rise and fall of the MB in Egypt. In Jordan and Kuwait, these groups were at the heart of wider protests for reform and political change that accompanied the early Arab Spring moments. They celebrated the electoral victory of the MB in Egypt and Tunisia but then suffered a popular and state backlash.

In Jordan, the wider population drew back from protest amid growing dismay about the missteps of MB rule in Egypt and grave concern about the disintegration of neighboring Syria in the wake of protests. In Kuwait, a similar pattern was also accompanied by a strong campaign by Saudi Arabia and the UAE to crack down on the MB in their own countries and to put pressure on Kuwait to do the same. Today both groups play a limited role, and tribal and pro-government groups have taken the majority of seats in parliament. Kuwait has long had a small but loud salafi political current that has engaged in electoral politics; the current secured four seats in the 2012 elections, out of 50, and two in 2014.

MB groups in Syria and Libya hoped to ride the anti-regime revolutions to political victory. But in both cases—as protests led to a shooting war, state collapse, and conditions of militia-dominated chaos—MB-affiliated groups have taken a back seat to more radical jihadi-salafi groups who are more adept at the use of extreme violence. In both Syria and Libya, the space for politics has been extinguished. In conditions of civil war, the more radical groups have proven more effectual.

> *In both Syria and Libya, the space for politics has been extinguished.*

Two regional backers, Qatar and Turkey, aided the upward momentum of the MB. Qatar's Al Jazeera had become the face and voice of the first wave of pro-democracy uprisings and had continued to be an avid communicator for the MB governments that won the first round of elections. Qatar backed this up with generous financial aid to the governments of Egypt and Tunisia and arms to the Islamist rebels in Libya and Syria. But Qatar was powerless to stop the uprising and coup against the MB in Egypt and the pressured resignation of the Ennahda government in Tunisia. And Qatar came under intense pressure from Saudi Arabia and its GCC partners to end or at least dramatically curtail its support for the MB. Although on a course different from its GCC neighbors, Doha has been forced to accept the new realities, curtail its support for the MB, and even ask a number of the MB's leaders to leave Doha.

As the Arab Spring unfolded, Turkish President Recep Tayyip Erdoğan seemed convinced that he, too, was on the right side of history and that the AKP model would be emulated throughout the Arab world. He welcomed MB victories in Egypt and Tunisia and reveled in a "victory tour" of Arab Spring countries in the fall of 2011. But his long shadow quickly shortened after the MB lost favor and power in Egypt, Ennahda had to step back in Tunisia, and his expectations of a quick rebel victory in Syria turned into a drawn-out civil war in which Bashar al-Assad and al Qaeda-affiliated terrorist groups ruled the day.

A Saudi/UAE/Sisi-led-Egypt alliance has emerged in place of the Turkey/Qatar/MB-led-Egypt trilateral alliance. Although Egypt and Saudi Arabia were on opposing sides of the MB issue in the 1960s, with Riyadh supporting the MB against Nasser's pan-Arab secular nationalism, they have now joined together to fight the group.

The MB continues to be part of political life in some Arab countries such as Morocco, Tunisia, and Yemen. But it is under strong repression in Egypt and the GCC and has lost ground to radical jihadists in Syria and Iraq. It will remain an important trend in Arab political life, but its political fortunes will vary dramatically from country to country based on the decisions of its local leaders and the conditions of each country.

For the non-jihadi salafi groups that have chosen to remain in the political realm, it remains to be seen whether they will be able to occupy some of the space ceded by the MB and whether they will be able to build bridges with other secular and nationalist sectors of society while maintaining a strict Islamist discourse.

On the jihadi-salafi side of the political Islamic spectrum, the ISG has risen to central prominence, overshadowing al Qaeda as a regional and global brand. Numerous groups pledged allegiance to the new caliphate including Ansar Beit al-Maqdis in Sinai, Ansar al-Shari'a in Yemen, Jund al-Khilafah in Algeria, in addition to fighters in Libya, Tunisia, and further afield in Nigeria, Pakistan, reaching all the way to the Abu Sayyaf group in the Philippines.

Radical jihadi groups have proved most effective at seizing territory in ungoverned spaces where state authority doesn't exercise control.

In ideological provenance, of course, there are historical links between the mainstream MB and the radical offshoots. The socio-religious movement founded by Hassan al-Banna in Egypt in the late 1920s was given a radical and militant reinterpretation by Sayyid Qutb while in an Egyptian jail in the 1960s. Ayman al-Zawahiri, a co-founder of al Qaeda, took it in a radical and violent direction. In other words, the Egyptian MB did give birth to more radical offshoots, but the main movement remained within the political camp, not presenting violence as the primary means to change society.

One mistake of the MB in power in Egypt is that it did not put enough distance between itself and these radical groups, blurring the line between the two approaches. When challenged politically and then by the military, it used the language of martyrdom and armed retaliation—perhaps exactly what the military hoped it would do—rather than political compromise. In any case, the mainstream MB and its radical offshoots are distinct movements and phenomena despite a complex history and set of relationships.

The major rise of jihadi-salafi groups has a different socio-strategic provenance. It was forged among a band of radical Islamic Arabs in the crucible of American and Gulf support to the jihadi resistance to Soviet occupation in Afghanistan of the 1980s and then catapulted to international fame through the events of September 11, 2001. The movement married radical Islamist ideology with effective fighting experience and ample funding. It found refuge first in the Taliban state of the 1990s. It then sought to sink roots wherever state authority was collapsing and ungoverned space was available. Despite al Qaeda's dispersion and small defeats, it spread as an idea through the Internet to susceptible youth or groups around the world and morphed into a decentralized network that could claim a presence from Morocco to the mountains of Pakistan and beyond.

Radical jihadi groups have proved most effective at seizing territory in ungoverned spaces where state authority doesn't exercise control. Today radical jihadi groups dominate swaths of territory in parts of Afghanistan, Pakistan, Yemen, Somalia, Sinai, Libya, and Mali. The biggest resurgence and conquest have been in Syria and Iraq, where the ISG has carved out a state-sized piece of territory astride the Syrian-Iraqi border. The ISG considers all other parties and movements, including the MB, woefully lacking in the proper piety and zeal.

The ISG has now eclipsed al Qaeda as the dark hero of an angry and disgruntled Muslim fringe around the world. Al Qaeda's model of launching occasional terrorist operations against Arab or Western targets has been supplanted by a much more tenacious model of conquering and holding territory and claiming to re-establish an Islamic caliphate, all the while slaughtering civilians, enslaving women, and reveling in the sadism of online beheadings.

Where state institutions exist, these groups can be battled and kept at the margins, as they do not represent social mainstream thinking. But the groups have a strong hold in areas where state authority is non-existent and particularly where Sunni communities have strong political and security grievances, as in present day Iraq and Syria. This radical strain is unlikely to be stamped out completely in our lifetime. But where state authority can be restored through fresh political compacts, the ISG's writ can be gradually sapped of its political energy and combatted by reconstituted state institutions.

CONCLUSION

It is impossible in a short essay to do justice to the vast and complex topic of political Islam's current trajectories. In this essay, I have focused mainly on the MB and its affiliates and the ISG and similar jihadi groups. I have not given equal space to the varied trajectory of salafi movements—some of which are part of the jihadi movement, others part of the MB, but many more charting an independent course. Nor have I examined the powerful role of militant Shi'ite Islamic groups such as Hezbollah and numerous Iraqi Shi'ite militias that have been buttressed by Iran and that have helped heighten sectarian tensions and tear apart the fabric of the Levant.

But for the mainstream MB and for the radical jihadi fringe, the past four years have been dramatic ones. The MB has proven most effective at mobilizing for elections while the radical jihadi fringe has done best mobilizing for civil wars. This partly reflects the declining appeal of nationalist and non-religious ideologies, which were able to mobilize parties, revolutions, and civil wars in the Middle East only a few decades ago. It also reflects the failure of non-religious groups to build strong grass roots and organize and communicate effectively.

But MB parties after elections have found that as political Islamic movements, unless they become more political and less Islamic, they will not be able to hold the center and hold on to power. Muslim populations are looking for parties to govern effectively, democratically, and fairly—not to tell them how to practice their religion. Radical jihadi groups are trying to take advantage of failed states to build states of their own. While they will find that they can exist at the margins, they are not able to build the sustained local support and external acceptance that could make their state projects viable.

In the recent past, political Islam seemed to be the future. Over the past four years, political Islamic movements have rampaged loudly through the political and armed conflicts of the Arab world. But they have failed to make the transition from their ideological base to the wider public, as the AKP did—at least for a while—in Turkey. And they failed to present a convincing example that they are ready to lead an inclusive polity or resolve a civil war.

But someone has to lead. The many disappointments—and small successes—of the past four years should spur leaders of mainstream political Islamic movements to examine the reasons for their reversals and recognize that general publics want better government services, not more religious governance.

More importantly, recent events should spur secular, nationalist, and other non-Islamist groups to examine the causes of their own weakness and redouble their efforts to organize, mobilize, and lead a movement of political renewal in the troubled Arab world. Meanwhile, the states and populations of the region have to keep up their fight against the ISG and al Qaeda and its affiliates, which thrive like a virus on the fevered dysfunctions of the status quo. They threaten not only regional and international security, but the very fabric of society for the millions of citizens in the Arab world who have clamored bravely for a more civic, free, just, and prosperous life. ■

5 Assessing the Islamic State Threat

STEPHEN D. BIDDLE

In early June 2014, Islamic State group (ISG) militants conquered the Iraqi city of Mosul, put to flight four Iraqi Army divisions, and continued south to within a few miles of Baghdad.[1] In the process, the ISG wrested control of a contiguous territory comprising much of northwestern Iraq and eastern Syria. These developments understandably focused intense attention on the group and its potential threat to Western interests.

To date, assessments of that threat have mostly been dire. U.S. Secretary of Defense Chuck Hagel described the ISG as "an imminent threat to every interest we have," a danger "greater than al Qaeda," and a peril "beyond anything that we've seen."[2] President Obama called the ISG a "savage organization" that poses a "significant threat" to the United States and its allies.[3] British Prime Minister David Cameron has called the group a "mor-

1. The Islamic State group (ISG) is known by several names, including ISIL (the Islamic State of Iraq and the Levant), ISIS (the Islamic State of Iraq and al Sham), and IS, or the Islamic State (reflecting its claim of state sovereignty over the territory it now controls).

2. See, e.g., Missy Ryan, "Islamic State threat 'beyond anything we've seen': Pentagon," Reuters, August 21, 2014, http://www.reuters.com/article/2014/08/21/us-usa-islamicstate-idUSKBN0GL24V20140821; Jeremy Herb, "Chuck Hagel: ISIL 'Beyond Anything that We've Seen,'" *Politico*, August 21, 2014, http://www.politico.com/story/2014/08/chuck-hagel-isil-defense-james-foley-110241.html.3.

3. Jim Garamone, "NATO Allies Agree ISIL Poses 'Significant Threat,' Obama Says," *DoD News*, September 5, 2014, http://www.defense.gov/news/newsarticle.aspx?id=123101.

tal threat."[4] Nor is this strictly a Western perspective. Iranian Foreign Minister Mohammad Javad Zarif said the ISG is "committing acts of horrendous genocide and crimes against humanity" and "needs to be tackled by the international community and by every country in the region."[5] And the Saudi Grand Mufti called the ISG "the greatest enemy of Islam."[6]

The ISG does indeed pose a threat to important Western interests. But the severity of that threat is smaller than one might suppose given the tenor of public debate to date. The fact is that the ISG threat to the West, while real, falls into an awkward middle ground between the vital and the negligible. Real but limited threats of this kind make for unusually difficult policymaking, and the result to date has been a U.S. strategy that has had great difficulty aligning ends and means.

This paper explains the three main Western interests the ISG threatens: homeland security, humanitarian concerns, and the health of the global economy.[7] This discussion uses U.S. homeland security and economics as a lens for understanding the ISG threat to the West generally. Though the magnitude of some threats varies across target states, these are differences in degree rather than kind. The overall assessment drawn for the United States below is broadly representative for Western nations as a group. This paper concludes by sketching some of the policy dilemmas created by the real but limited scale of the threat the ISG poses to these interests.

HOMELAND SECURITY

Perhaps the most widely discussed danger the ISG poses is its potential to mount terrorist attacks against the United States or its allies. The ISG is clearly no friend of the West and deploys several thousand foreign fighters in Syria and Iraq. Some hold Western passports and could return as terrorists. The terrorism peril posed by the ISG is real and governments cannot ignore it.

But that danger needs to be kept in context. ISG terrorism is not a threat to any Western nation's way of life. A major terrorist attack would pose grave political risks for any elected official on whose watch it occurred. And the ISG's foreign fighters pose a greater threat than many such groups. But without weapons of mass destruction, the risks the ISG poses to life and property outside the Middle East are limited.

4. John Aglionby and Geoff Dyer, "David Cameron vows action over 'mortal threat' from Isis," *Financial Times*, September 25, 2014, http://www.ft.com/cms/s/0/f0179b3e-4480-11e4-bce8-00144feabdc0.html#axzz3OSG0GPZD.
5. U.S. Institute of Peace, "Iran's Leaders on Iraq Crisis and ISIS," October 16, 2014, http://iranprimer.usip.org/blog/2014/oct/16/irans-leaders-iraq-crisis-and-isis.
6. Frank Gardner, "Islamic State sets sights on Saudi Arabia," *BBC News*, November 14, 2014, http://www.bbc.com/news/world-europe-30061109.
7. For actors in the region, the stability of states such as Jordan, Turkey, Iran, Saudi Arabia, and the other members of the GCC is obviously a critical interest in its own right. For others, regional stability's importance derives chiefly from its instrumental value in promoting underlying interests in homeland security, humanitarian concern, and economic health. Below I consider the danger of contagion by which the conflict with the ISG might spread to other states in the region, but I do so through the lens of these underlying primary concerns.

In fact, terrorism has never posed existential costs to any Western state, nor has terrorism ever been a major contributor to aggregate morbidity-and-mortality in any Western society. Even in 2001, the most lethal year in U.S. history for deaths of U.S. citizens due to terrorist attack, more Americans died of peptic ulcers than died of terrorism; in the years since then, more Americans have been killed by deer than by international terrorists.[8] Even post-1948 Israel has never seen a year in which terrorists killed more citizens than auto accidents did.[9] And for now, the U.S. intelligence community has assessed that the ISG in fact poses no imminent threat of terrorist attacks on U.S. soil.[10] For the foreseeable future, the ISG has its hands full waging its own existential war with its "near enemies"—the governments of Iraq and Syria and a variety of hostile militias and other local non-state actors.

Even post-1948 Israel has never seen a year in which terrorists killed more citizens than auto accidents did.

Of course, this does not mean that the ISG could never pose such threats in the future, especially if unchallenged by U.S. or other counterterrorist efforts. The limited damage terrorists have inflicted on the West to date is due in part to Western counterterrorism efforts; limited damage to date does not necessarily mean the U.S. can safely stand down or ignore terrorism altogether. And even a threat with limited objective lethality can pose vexing political problems: classical terrorist strategy is designed to create widespread fear through limited but lurid killing. Managing this fear without overreacting is a major challenge for Western governments. Terrorism thus cannot simply be ignored, and the ISG in particular poses a terrorist threat that U.S. policy must address in some way. But an important component of sound counterterrorism policy is to calm the typically exaggerated fears

---

8. On fatalities from peptic ulcers in 2001, see Elizabeth Arias et al., "Deaths: Final Data for 2001," *CDC National Vital Statistics Reports* 52, no. 3 (September 18, 2003), Table 10; for comparisons of terrorism and other sources of morbidity and mortality in U.S. society generally, see John Mueller and Mark G. Stewart, "Hardly Existential: Thinking Rationally about Terrorism," *Foreign Affairs,* April 2010, http://www.foreignaffairs.com/articles/66186/john-mueller-and-mark-g-stewart/hardly-existential.

9. Data on Israeli fatalities from terrorist attacks are compiled by Israel's Ministry of Foreign Affairs and Trade, available at http://mfa.gov.il/mfa/Pages/default.aspx. Even during 2002, when Israel experienced its highest number of terrorism-related fatalities (452 in total), 456 people died on the road. See Central Bureau of Statistics, *Road Accidents With Casualties: General Summaries 2002,* Jerusalem, June 2003, http://www.cbs.gov.il/publications/acci02/acci02e.pdf.

10. Statement of Secretary of Defense Chuck Hagel before the Senate Armed Services Committee, September 16, 2014, http://www.washingtonpost.com/world/national-security/transcript-hagel-testifies-to-the-senate-armed-services-committee-on-the-islamic-state/2014/09/16/a4909e26-3dab-11e4-b0ea-8141703bbf6f_story.html.

such threats create and to respond without overreaction that causes the counterterrorist cure to be worse than the disease. The real homeland security challenge in the ISG for the West is thus one of political management. In objective terms, ISG terrorism is not an existential danger to Western societies, and the ISG's other threats may pose greater perils for Western interests.

HUMANITARIAN CONCERNS

The humanitarian stakes in the Syrian and Iraqi civil wars are enormous. The Iraq war will probably look much like Syria's soon and may in time look a lot like Iraq itself circa 2006. In Syria more than 50,000 civilians already have died, with no end in sight; in Iraq more than 120,000 were killed between 2003 and 2011.[11] Wars of this kind are notoriously difficult to terminate and typically drag on for years. Of 128 civil wars fought between 1945 and 2004, only one-fourth ended within two years. Datasets vary slightly with war definitions and other details, but most put the median duration of such wars at seven to ten years. An important minority of conflicts drags on for a generation or more.[12] A renewed Iraq war of seven to ten years' duration could easily produce another 100,000 innocent lives lost while Syrian fatalities continue apace. The West has not often intervened militarily in civil wars on purely humanitarian grounds. But the scale of potential suffering here is large, and far worse could be in store if the wars in Iraq and Syria spread.

Historically, civil wars of this kind often spill across borders. Of 142 civil wars fought between 1950 and 1999, fully 61 saw major military intervention by neighboring states at some point.[13] Even more common is subversion, wherein states weaken rivals by supporting insurgency to kindle civil warfare.[14] The wars in Iraq and Syria may be especially vulnerable to such contagion dynamics given the deep Sunni-Shi'ite fault line running throughout the region, the regional proxy war already ongoing between Sunni Saudi Arabia and Shi'ite Iran, and the continuing spillover from Syria into its neighbors. Of course a truly regional war would require many infections; it is not the likeliest outcome.

---

11. Fatality data are drawn from https://www.iraqbodycount.org and Laia Balcells, Lionel Beehner and Jonah Schulhofer-Wohl, "How Should We Count the War Dead in Syria?" *Washington Post Monkey Cage* (blog), May 1, 2014, http://www.washingtonpost.com/blogs/monkey-cage/wp/2014/05/01/how-should-we-count-the-war-dead-in-syria.
12. James D. Fearon, "Why Do Some Civil Wars Last So Much Longer Than Others?" *Journal of Peace Research* 41, no. 3 (May 2004): 275–302; Christopher Paul et al., *Paths to Victory: Lessons from Modern Insurgencies* (Washington, DC: RAND, 2013); David Cunningham, "Veto Players and Civil War Duration," *American Journal of Political Science* 50, no. 4 (October 2006): 875–892; David Collier, "Duration of Civil War," *Journal of Peace Research* 41, no. 3 (2004): 253–273.
13. Data are drawn from Stephen Biddle, Jeffrey Friedman, and Stephen Long, "Civil War Intervention and the Problem of Iraq," *International Studies Quarterly* 56, no. 1 (March 2012): 85–98; replication files are posted at http://scholar.harvard.edu/files/friedman/files/bfl_isq_data.zip. Note that these data use a less restrictive domain definition than those documented in note 2, thus including a larger number of lower-intensity conflicts as civil wars. This is conservative with respect to the intervention rate cited above, as intervention rates are typically higher in higher-intensity conflicts—hence the less-intense conflicts included in the data underlying the rate above would tend to depress that rate relative to a sample comprising more-intense wars; the sample in note 2 would thus presumably yield a higher intervention rate than the 43 percent figure (61 of 142 wars) cited above.
14. Idean Salehyan, "The Delegation of War to Rebel Organizations," *Journal of Conflict Resolution* 54, no. 3 (2010): 493–515.

But it cannot safely be excluded, the risk grows the longer the war drags on, and if the conflict does spread, even partially, the consequences multiply accordingly.[15] It is not beyond the realm of possibility that a region-wide version of today's Syrian and Iraqi wars could eventually approach the Rwandan genocide in the number of innocent lives lost, albeit over a much longer period.[16]

A region-wide version of today's Syrian and Iraqi wars could eventually approach the Rwandan genocide in the number of innocent lives lost.

ECONOMIC RISK

Finally, there are economic stakes. Western economic exposure to Gulf oil shocks may be declining as efficiency improves, oil prices fall, and North American shale oil and gas develop. But serious risks will remain for the foreseeable future. Oil is a fungible, globally traded commodity. Regardless of the source of any given state's consumption, any major reduction in world supply will increase prices to the United States, to the West, and to their trading partners, especially if the change is sudden. A serious reduction in Gulf production would be a globally significant economic threat.

The cost, however, varies with the war's extent and duration. A seven-year war that cut Iraqi output to 2006 levels but did not spread and did not affect other Gulf exporters' production would remove one million barrels a day (mbd) from world supply. There are many uncertainties in estimating effects from oil shocks, but the best available analysis suggests that this might increase world oil prices by eight to ten percent. If so, the best available macroeconomic analysis suggests that the result could cut U.S. gross domestic product by four-tenths of a percentage point; effects on other Western economies would vary as a function of their respective energy intensities, but many would be similar.[17] This would be regrettable, but manageable.

15. A statistical analysis conducted before the outbreak of civil war in Syria assessed a greater than 20 percent probability that a renewed war in Iraq would spread beyond its borders to two or more neighboring states if Iraqi warfare lasted five years or more; arguably the current fighting in Iraq represents an initial stage in this process of contagion already, which would imply that the odds of further spread are now higher. See Biddle, Friedman, and Long, "Civil War Intervention and the Problem of Iraq," at 94–96.

16. The 1994 Rwandan genocide killed at least 500,000 Tutsis; for a discussion of casualty estimates, see Alan J. Kuperman, *The Limits of Humanitarian Intervention: Genocide in Rwanda* (Washington, DC: Brookings, 2001).

17. Kenneth R. Vincent, "The Economic Costs of Persian Gulf Oil Supply Disruptions," in Charles L. Glaser and Rosemary A. Kelanic, eds., *Crude Calculus: Reexamining the Energy Logic of the U.S. Military Commitment to the Persian Gulf* (Stanford University Press, forthcoming).

By contrast, a region-wide war that cut oil production by 50 percent across the Gulf Cooperation Council (GCC) could remove 13 mbd or nearly 15 percent of worldwide production. Such a reduction would be a very different story. It would exceed the largest previous Gulf oil shock (the 1973-1974 OPEC embargo) by nearly a factor of four; the best available analysis suggests this might double world oil prices, cutting U.S. gross domestic product by three to five percentage points.[18] At 2014 levels, this would imply $450-750 billion a year in lost U.S. economic output, which could easily tip the U.S. economy into recession, depending on conditions at the time. With broadly similar effects elsewhere, the effect on the global economy could be severe.

Gulf states' pipelines, pumping stations, and other oil infrastructure offer a natural target.

A long civil war in Iraq and Syria would threaten just such a reduction. Insurgents have strong incentives to weaken rivals by targeting their war-supporting economy. Gulf states' pipelines, pumping stations, and other oil infrastructure offer a natural target. In fact oil's war-supporting potential is a major incentive for contagion in the Gulf: a classical strategy for weakening rivals in civil warfare is to embroil their external patrons in civil wars of their own by fomenting unrest there. Inasmuch as the Sunni-Shi'ite fault line that constitutes the primary casus belli in both Iraq and Syria runs throughout the region and across all the GCC's major oil producers, there are many possible incentives for actors in a long war to strike at war-supporting oil infrastructure beyond their borders.

The United States hopes that the ISG's radicalism will enable a new, stable, regional coalition to be formed among conservative powers of all sects and ethnicities; perhaps this will succeed, but maintaining such a polyglot alliance will be a major diplomatic challenge. And if it fails, incentives will grow over time to pursue sectarian agendas via proxy warfare that will turn the GCC's oil infrastructure into an increasingly attractive target. A natural strategy for weakening anti-Bashar al-Assad Sunni rebels in Syria, for example, would be for Assad or Shi'ite allies of Assad's to foment unrest in Saudi Arabia's Eastern Province, embroiling the support base for Sunni rebels in a civil war of its own that would drain resources from Saudi proxies abroad. Or a deepening proxy war could persuade Iran to escalate by closing the Strait of Hormuz to weaken its Sunni foes. Sunnis face similar incentives versus Shi'ite infrastructure, and such dangers imperil every state in the region to at least some degree.

Even a long war, however, does not imply a certainty of regional contagion and its

18. Ibid.

associated economic consequences. The war may not spread, and even a war that spreads might not engulf the entire region. A localized war with a limited effect on Iraqi production would pose much smaller stakes, and if it does spread, Gulf states may be willing to forgo attacks on one another's oil infrastructure given their mutual vulnerability.

And even the worst case, bad as it would be, would not be another Great Depression. A region-wide war that cost the U.S. economy $450-750 billion a year in lost output would be a setback of major proportions, with real economic suffering throughout the West and beyond. But the normal economic cycle regularly produces output swings in excess of three to five percentage points in GDP: the effects would be bad, but they would not mean the end of today's way of life in any Western state.

POLICY IMPLICATIONS

Taken together, these stakes are thus real—but not existential. Of them, the economic stake poses the most severe direct threat to objective Western hard security interests. And this stake is indeed serious: the worst case scenario of a region-wide Sunni-Shi'a war catalyzed by the ISG could cause widespread economic contraction across the West. But the worst case is not the likeliest one. And even the worst case would fall far short of a new Great Depression. The net result is a war that is too important to ignore, but not important enough to warrant total commitment or unlimited liability.

Given a conflict with real but limited stakes for Westerners, the natural instinct of many elected officials is to seek some real but limited way to wage it. Limited strategies are attractive as reactions to limited Western stakes, but they often fail in wars against faraway enemies for whom the stakes are far higher. For Iraqis, Syrians, Saudis, Iranians, and others in the region, the wars in Iraq and Syria are potentially existential. Humanitarian stakes that Westerners may choose to overlook are catastrophes for the societies who bear them. Conflicts that Westerners may see as potential sources of contagion are actual threats of genocidal warfare to local populations. Potential regime changes may be matters of real but limited consequence to Westerners but are matters of life and death for the regimes themselves and their supporters.

This does not mean that regional powers will opt for total war to protect potentially existential stakes; bet-hedging and partial deal-making are natural strategies for limiting risk. Many in the region will prefer these as initial responses. For many states in the region, the ISG also poses a complex array of often conflicting interests and incentives.

- Turkey sees the ISG as a potential threat but also opposes Assad and is wary of the Syrian Kurdish militias that fight both Assad and the ISG.
- Saudi Arabia opposes the ISG but also Assad and is deeply skeptical about the Iraqi government's alliance with Iran against the ISG.
- Iran opposes the ISG, favors Assad, and has been locked in a proxy war against the same Saudi Arabia that also opposes the ISG.

These cross-cutting interests, many of them seen as vital by the actors in the region, pose extraordinary challenges for maintaining a unified coalition to share burdens and reduce the cost of action for Western states whose interests are more limited. There are many reasons to be skeptical that limited Western efforts will succeed in any simple or straightforward way in a long conflict involving local actors whose sometimes conflicting interests often outstrip Westerners'.

In fact, the real options open to Western leaders in limited-stakes conflicts of this kind are typically unattractive. Limited efforts seem to fit the stakes, but often fail to secure them. Greater exertions may secure the stake but at a price that often exceeds the value of the interests at risk. Staying out altogether cuts the state's losses but sacrifices stakes that are real even if they fall short of the existential.

This dilemma underlies much of the incoherence in the U.S. debate. Senior U.S. administration officials describe the ISG's threat in grave terms that imply serious stakes. Yet the president has precluded any major U.S. ground force deployment. Instead he holds that this grave threat can be met with a limited program of airstrikes, aid, and diplomatic isolation that even he implies cannot do more than shorten a very long war into one perhaps a few years shorter. Conservative critics attack the administration for precluding options such as U.S. ground combat deployments, but many fewer voices call for actually sending a ground force that could destroy the ISG any time soon. Polling suggests the U.S. public supports military action against the ISG. But the same polls suggest that U.S. voters doubt this action will succeed.[19] Real but limited stakes tend to create this kind of ambivalence and the cognitive dissonance that often accompanies it. But this is what the ISG challenge presents: the stakes for the West here lie in the awkward middle ground between the vital and the irrelevant. And that is going to continue to make for a difficult series of policy dilemmas for a long time to come. ■

19. See, e.g., "Voters Think Iraq May Already Be Lost," *Rasmussen Reports*, August 11, 2014, http://www.rasmussenreports.com/public_content/politics/issues/voters_think_iraq_may_already_be_lost.

6 Iran Inside and Out

FARIDEH FARHI

The unfolding crisis in Iraq and Syria has brought to the fore a debate over other countries' relationships with Iran. Regional actors and their Western allies share some interests with Iran in Iraq, but they are hostile to the role Iran plays in Syria and Lebanon and critical of its alleged machinations in Yemen. At the same time, since the election of President Hassan Rouhani in 2013, Iran has also made an effort to renew and improve relations with its Gulf neighbors, the region, and beyond. Distinct from the question of whether and how to engage Iran is the question of the underlying dynamics that shape Iran's position and choices in the region.

Iran does not hide its aspiration for regional prominence. The "20-Year Outlook" document released in the last year of the reformist Mohammad Khatami's presidency makes Tehran's objectives clear.[1] The document outlines a road map for the country's economic, political, social, and cultural developments. It calls for an Iran that will be an "inspiring model" for the Islamic world and in "the top economic, scientific and technological position in Southwest Asia (including Central Asia, Caucasus, the Middle East, and neighboring countries)" by 2025. Its vitality persists, with Iranians continuing to call it the "guiding document" ten years after its issuance.

1. The Persian text of the document can be found via the following link: Mohammed Khatami, "Iran 20-Year Outlook," http://old.maslahat.ir/Contents.aspx?p=67ee04aa-7171-4f72-bdf7-e6f68c3547e5.

The economic and political effects of global sanctions, aggravated by plummeting oil prices, are undermining those lofty ambitions, as are the continuing domestic institutional struggles within Iran. While the government has been able to make some adjustments and has made some steps toward stability, tensions remain among the power elite and between the government and the electorate. How quickly and well the governance structure addresses these issues will have a major impact on whether the country can play the leading role that the Iranians aspire to and whether it can remain an island of relative stability in a regional sea of political chaos.

How quickly and well the governance structure addresses these issues will have a major impact on whether the country can play the leading role that the Iranians aspire to and whether it can remain an island of relative stability in a regional sea of political chaos.

A VOLATILE REGION

Events of recent years have highlighted the relationship between Iran's domestic politics—including its institutions and the role of economic policy—and its regional clout and aspirations. The country has struggled internally since the tumultuous period between 2009 and 2011 revealed just how contested its political system had become. In addition, like other regional powers, Iran's leaders have appeared unsure of how to react to rapid political developments. Leader Seyyed Ali Khamenei first applauded the Arab Spring, terming it an "Islamic Awakening." More recently, Iran has swung into an anti-revolutionary mode in the name of regional security and stability, supporting the governments of Syria and Iraq against their insurgencies. Tehran also dispatched its deputy foreign minister for Arab and African affairs to attend General Abdel-Fattah al-Sisi's inauguration in Egypt in June 2014, a year after the army pushed aside an elected Islamist government.

Similarly, since the election of President Hassan Rouhani in 2013, Iran has tried to renew and improve relations with its Arab Gulf neighbors, the region, and beyond, and it could benefit from interests in Iraq it shares with regional actors and their Western allies. Yet these same actors continue to find threatening Tehran's increasing influence in Iraq through its coordination of Shi'ite militias to fight the Islamic State group (ISG), the role it plays supporting the Bashar al-Assad regime in Syria and Hezbollah in Lebanon, as well as its alleged machinations in Yemen.

Much of this threat perception can be traced to the underlying consistency that characterizes Iran's foreign and security policy, despite pivots depending on who has taken the presidential helm. This underlying consistency, in turn, stems from the evolution of Iran's institutions, which give stability top priority. They have served as a bulwark against dramatically shifting fortunes for the last three decades while providing arenas in which deep differences of opinion about Iran's relationship to the region and the world are negotiated. Without a doubt, Iran is feeling its way in the midst of a disintegrating regional architecture while facing a ruinous sanctions regime but is doing so by relying on institutions and decisionmaking processes that have become increasingly robust and developed in the face of international pressures that the country has been under since its revolution.

More recently, Iran got a boost from the sudden emergence of the ISG and its recognition as a dangerous global phenomenon. That has placed Iran's policies toward Syria and Iraq in a different light, helping the country's regional position and posture. The Iranian foreign policy and security establishment can now boast that its warnings regarding Syria's "destabilization project" by the United States and regional powers such as Saudi Arabia and Turkey have proven prescient. It can also argue that its foreign policy is the most consistent in the region: pursuing systemic stability against brutal and destabilizing anti-systemic forces of terror.

That said, the Islamic Republic is still struggling to figure out how to punch at least close to its weight—in keeping with its revolutionary legacy, geographic size, and developed infrastructural links to the Gulf, South and Central Asia, and the Caucasus. Iran also has immense resources, a dynamic culture, and a highly educated population. To operate in its weight class, however, will require a nuclear accord that reverses long-standing policies intended to isolate Iran politically and pressure it economically. Furthermore, Iran can sustain this enhanced prominence only if it can keep its house in order. That is a tall order, and the peaceful management of the country's highly contested domestic politics is key to a stable Iran with or without a nuclear agreement.

DOMESTIC INSTITUTIONS

Maintaining stability in Iran over the past three decades has been an enormous challenge. Iran has gone through a historical revolution, a destructive war that lasted eight years, an unprecedented economic chokehold, and political tumults during the presidencies of both Khatami and Mahmoud Ahmadinejad. Yet it has not succumbed to the violent divisions and civil wars that have swept the neighborhood. Furthermore, it has survived and arguably prospered by relying on institutions established in both pre- and postrevolutionary times. They are deep enough to continue functioning, even if not efficiently, in the midst of extreme pressure, and flexible enough to adapt to changing circumstances.

To be sure, the increasingly complex institutional decisionmaking process has not been the only element of power for the Iranian state. Brute force and periodic crackdowns have also been powerful instruments of control. But these crackdowns, while showing force at any given moment, have not necessarily fortified the state. Instead, they have displayed that Iran's political leaders are more fearful of domestic challenges than external ones and exhibited a sense of vulnerability. More significantly, these crackdowns have not led to a militarized or police state. In 2013, an established political institution and process—an election—brought the country back from the highly polarized brink to which the disputed 2009 election and Ahmadinejad's unorthodox managerial practices and style had taken the country. Rouhani shares Ahmadinejad's elevated sense of Iran's strategic importance and significance as an indispensable power in the region and independent force in the world. But Rouhani differs significantly in his analysis of how to preserve Iran's security, counter its isolation, and improve its standing in the region and world. These differences in foreign policy outlooks are deep.[2] Their management in ways that have not torn the country apart can be explained only through the institutions that the Islamic Republic has been able to build.

In the national security arena, external pressures and threats have helped institution building. Consider the Supreme National Security Council (SNSC), which brings together officials from different institutions with different outlooks to debate and make decisions on how to respond to external threats and pressures. The SNSC has transformed the country's foreign policy decisionmaking process from the one-man rule of the prerevolutionary era to a more collective and interactive enterprise. Major policy shifts, including cooperation with the United States in Afghanistan and improved relations with Saudi Arabia during the Khatami era, could not have happened without discussions within the SNSC and eventual buy-in from across the political spectrum. The latest example of institutional decisionmaking was displayed in relation to Iraq after the ISG's takeover of Mosul. The SNSC managed differences of opinion over what to do and eventually different elements of Iran's approach—political and military. To be sure, tasks were delegated. The SNSC secretary, Ali Shamkhani, coordinated Iran's response to Iraq's domestic political dynamics, which eventually led to exertion of pressure for

2. For a discussion of competing foreign policy outlooks see Farideh Farhi and Saideh Lotfian, "Iran's Post-Revolution Foreign Policy Puzzle," in *Worldviews of Aspiring Powers: Domestic Foreign Policy Debates in China, India, Iran, Japan, and Russia*, Henry R. Nau and Deepa M. Ollapally, eds. (Oxford: Oxford University Press, 2012), 114–145.

the removal of Prime Minister Nouri al-Maliki.[3] The foreign ministry managed the relationship with the Kurdistan Regional Government,[4] and the Iran Revolutionary Guard Corps Qods forces oversaw military support.[5]

The SNSC also debated questions about the extent of Iran's involvement in attacks against the ISG and coordination through officials in Baghdad of the logistics of the U.S. attacks against the ISG in Iraq. Rouhani chairs the SNSC, and on significant security issues, he must also have the agreement of the Leader. But not even Khamenei's opinions on what should be done were generated independently of this process. He has the last word, but the decisionmaking process and elected officials who end up in the SNSC help shape and refine policy.[6]

Similar dynamics are at play for economic policymaking, traditionally the purview of the executive branch, its economy-related ministries, and their interaction with the parliament. This interaction has been fraught with conflict and has not been the most productive in terms of consistency and efficacy. Rampant corruption, unaccountable government officials, ideological decisionmaking, and the existence of many nontransparent parastatal institutions have been integral elements of the Islamic Republic.[7] At the same time, the Iranian state—which according to the latest figures employs 16.9 percent of the country's labor force—has managed to expand its economic reach in terms of welfare, regulatory, and increasingly even extractive capacities in support of national objectives.[8]

This reach now includes a nationwide registration system for identification cards relied on for all economic transactions, a computerized gasoline ration system, and monthly cash grants directly deposited in people's bank accounts. Information gathered from these registrations and the institution of a value-added tax system in 2008 have gradually been used to expand government revenue from

---

3. Loveday Morris, "A Letter from Sistani Turned the Tide against Iraq's Leader," *Washington Post*, August 13, 2014, http://www.washingtonpost.com/world/middle_east/a-letter-from-sistani-turned-the-tide-against-iraqs-leader/2014/08/13/3b3426cf-60ee-4856-ad26-d01a9c6cc9c3_story.html.
4. "Barzani Stresses Full Support for the New Iraqi Government," *Fars News Agency*, August 26, 2014, http://english.farsnews.com/newstext.aspx?nn=13930604001337.
5. Bozorgmehr Sharafedin, "Iran's Qasem Soleimani Wields Power behind the Scenes in Iraq," *BBC Persian*, June 17, 2014, http://www.bbc.com/news/world-middle-east-27883162.
6. Out of the 12 standing members of the SNSC, positions that can directly or indirectly change with elections include that of the president, the speaker of the parliament, the cabinet member in charge of budget and planning, and ministers of foreign affairs, interior, and intelligence. The president also appoints the secretary of the SNSC.
7. See, for instance, Jahangir Amuzegar, "Iran's 20-year Economic Perspective: Promises and Pitfalls," *Middle East Policy Council* 16, no. 3 (2009): 41–57.
8. Statistical Center of Iran, *Labor Force Data for the Summer of 1393*, 2014, http://www.amar.org.ir/Portals/0/Files/fulltext/1393/n_ank_93-2.pdf.

nonoil sources.[9] To be sure, the attempt to reduce reliance on oil revenues was halted, even reversed, during the Ahmadinejad years largely due to his expensive populist policies, which required enormous oil revenues generated by high prices. But the sanctions regime and rapid drop in oil prices have forced reversals of expansionary budgets and institutional changes that Ahmadinejad made, and they were accomplished without much bureaucratic challenge. For instance, Rouhani has reinstated the Management and Planning Organization as the body responsible for preparing the country's yearly budget along with medium- and long-term development plans and policies. Ahmadinejad dissolved this institution, which was established in the early years of Mohammad Reza Shah's regime. Rouhani then resurrected elements of it within his executive authority, combining it with another organization in charge of government administration and hiring.[10] With the reversal, this institution again returned to its focus on budget and planning. Whether this change will help turn around the ailing Iranian economy is unclear, but it is an example of how the country's deliberative and administrative institutions adjust to help the economy limp along in the face of the sanctions regime.

ARCHITECTURE OF POWER AND INSTITUTIONAL TENSIONS

The government adjusts despite deep tensions among the country's institutions. It is worth mentioning two institutions in particular—elections and the office of the Leader—designed to manage or moderate political competition, conflicts, and systemic contradictions. Their failure to perform their tasks proved disastrous in 2009, while their adjustments became a source of stability in 2013.

The combined presidential and municipal council elections of 2013 were the thirty-first election in the 35-year history of the Islamic Republic.[11] Elections have been the method of choice for managing popular participation, socializing the newer generations into the Islamic Republic, and regulating and ultimately negotiating inter-relite competition. In 2009, electoral politics failed in all these objectives. The significance of the 2013 election lies less in the election of a centrist president and more in the reaffirmation of the legitimacy, value, and functionality of this foundational institution.

Recent changes in electoral cycles include turning them into biannual affairs through

9. The Islamic Republic's extractive capacity is still very low in comparison to, for instance, its nonoil producing neighbor Turkey. According to the head of Iran's tax organization, the weight of taxation only falls on 40 percent of the country's gross domestic product. The rest—including large religious and economic foundations—either fail to pay taxes or are not required to. But again, the sanctions regime and the rapid drop in oil prices have forced the state to seek more taxes. The government has announced its intention to broaden the base for nonoil tax revenues from six to ten percent of the Gross Domestic Product. International Monetary Fund, *Islamic Republic of Iran: IMF Country Report No.14/93*, April 2014, http://www.imf.org/external/pubs/ft/scr/2014/cr1493.pdf.

10. This was established in 1948 and originally named the Plan Organization, then the Plan and Budget Organization. Ahmadinejad disbanded it in 2007.

11. That includes the three founding elections held in the immediate postrevolution years regarding the change of regime, the election of Constitutional Assembly, and the approval of the Islamic Constitution.

the aggregation of various elections. Elections previously accentuated political competition when they were held almost every year. The slower pace helped rationalize the electoral process. All the same, the problem of who and which political forces can participate in the electoral process remains. That undoubtedly will become a source of tension and conflict unless the conservative Guardian Council, which vets candidates, makes a further adjustment and allows a broader spectrum of candidates to run for office. If it cannot, then it will continue to keep the Islamic Republic vulnerable to and hobbled by periodic and unpredictable outbursts. The security forces of the Islamic Republic may be able to continue to control crowds dissatisfied with electoral outcomes. But the systemic inability to quiet the Iranian political elite's dissatisfaction with the rules of game will assure dysfunction of a political system paralyzed by intense procedural disagreements at the top.

Meanwhile, the office of the Leader poses two problems for the future of the Islamic Republic. The first concerns the length of the term of the occupant, which is effectively for life. The second relates to the question of transition in that office after years of power aggregated by the person who holds that office. Not surprisingly, lack of rotation has proved a recipe for accumulation of power and expansion of reach of the person who occupies that office. While many observers of Iran tend to reduce the Leader's office to the personality and ideological orientation of the office holder, the much deeper problem is constitutional. The Iranian constitution has created two executives, one of which effectively has a life term while the other changes every eight years (and potentially even every four years). Rotation of the Leader is possible only in case of death or mental or physical incapacity to perform constitutional duties as determined by the Council of Experts.[12]

This does not mean that the president—explicitly identified in the constitution as the second most important person after the Leader—lacks substantial power. In fact, the powers of the elected president include the power of the purse and control of the government's vast bureaucracy. Those powers spawned the deepest conflicts of the country, first in the early years of the Islamic Republic and then in the second term of Ahmadinejad's presidency. Unless these two executives find a way to work with each other, their conflicts are bound to reverberate up and down the institutions of the Islamic Republic.

The problem lies in the constitutional ambiguity that exists regarding the two executives' power and authority. The Leader is the commander-in-chief, appoints

12. Constitution of the Islamic Republic, Article 112, http://www.iranonline.com/iran/iran-info/government/constitution.html.

key civilian and military officials, and determines the general policies and direction of the Islamic Republic. He can also step in to resolve conflicts among the three branches of government. He can delegate the resolution of conflicts that cannot be addressed through "normal" means to the Expediency Council.

At the same time, Article 113 gives the responsibility for implementing the Constitution to the president except in matters directly concerning the office of the Leader. The president sets general policies, makes appointments, and investigates violations of citizens' constitutional rights. To be sure, the latter power may be academic in a country where the judiciary and security forces routinely violate citizen's rights. But these issues sometimes concern the rights and treatment of long-standing officials of the Islamic Republic, such as the unconstitutional house arrests of former Prime Minister Mir Hossein Mussavi and former Speaker of the Parliament Mehdi Karrubi. When such incidents become part of public conversation, they can become sources of great friction. That is especially true when during Khamenei's long rule, he increasingly has encroached on the powers and authority of the president in the name of "general interest of the state."

Without a reversal of this process, the tensions from the encroachments will become even more blatant. Even assuming a smooth transition to a new Leader, made possible by a selection process in the Council of Experts, the power that a long-serving Leader can amass is bound to be challenged during the transition to a successor. At the end of the day, if the country becomes too accustomed to the discretion of the long-standing occupant of the office, a change of occupant will unsettle the office. That could affect Iran domestically and its regional aspirations. The office's pivotal role in the political set-up of the Islamic Republic makes it imperative to delineate and make legitimate its powers before the next transition.

CONCLUSION: IMPLICATIONS FOR IRAN'S REGIONAL ROLE

During his presidency, Ahmadinejad polarized Iran and sharpened tensions with countries around the world. In 2013, Iran relied on established political institutions to bring the country back from the brink. Many in the international community viewed this as a positive development. Since then, the Rouhani administration has aimed at renewing and improving bonds with Iran's Gulf neighbors and the international community more broadly. The response to this effort has been mixed. Some see opportunity for improved relations and possible collaboration, while others remain concerned and question the sustainability of recent diplomatic efforts given Iran's highly contested political environment.

The postrevolutionary Iranian elite has always had competing and conflicting views on what Iranian foreign policy should look like and how to implement it. Fault lines exist regarding Iran's relationship to the global order, the role of the government in promoting economic justice, and cultural and religious values. There are also foundational disagreements about the proper rules for politics and whether the republican or Islamic aspects of the Islamic Republic should have more weight. It is unlikely that any of these differences and the forces that align on different sides of the issues will go away. Still, decades of turmoil have not turned the Iranian state into a militarized nation or security state. Political institutions still matter—indeed, they have become increasingly important.

> *Events of the past few years suggest that Iran's political institutions, more than its polarizing personalities, will determine Iran's ability to define and pursue successful policies at home and abroad.*

Iran's government aspires to a role as the leading player in its neighborhood. Whether the United States will agree to abandon its three-decade policy of containing Iran will make a difference in the speed with which the Islamic Republic can pursue its stated aspiration to rise as the leading regional player. Equally if not more important, however, is the ability of the Iranian political system to pursue a direction that retains a level of healthy competitiveness and manages internal discord stemming from the nation's diverse interests and changing sentiments. Events of the past few years suggest that Iran's political institutions, more than its polarizing personalities, will determine Iran's ability to define and pursue successful policies at home and abroad. ■

7 Maghreb Rising: Competition and Realignment

HAIM MALKA

After decades on the margins of the Arab world, what happens in North Africa's Maghreb region now reaches into its core.[1] The "Arab West" captured attention in December 2010 when thousands of Tunisians took to the streets to protest former president Zine el-Abidine Ben Ali's repressive rule. Those demonstrations sent shockwaves across the region and inspired millions of Arabs in Egypt, Syria, Bahrain, Yemen, and elsewhere to rise up against authoritarian rulers.

Since December 2010 much has changed. Libya is divided by civil war and is destabilizing its neighbors, political Islamists won elections in Morocco, and Tunisia is on a fragile path toward more representative government after decades of dictatorship. These trends, combined with regional uncertainty, turmoil, and competition, increasingly affect the interests of a wide range of actors. No longer an outlier, the Maghreb is now an important strategic component of new regional alignments that have been coalescing since the uprisings.

The United Arab Emirates (UAE), Qatar, and Turkey have been the most assertive outside actors in the Maghreb. These gov-

1. The Maghreb is defined here as the states of Morocco, Algeria, Tunisia, and Libya.

ernments seek to reshape regional alliances to protect national interests—and their hold on power. They desire deeper military, diplomatic, and economic partnerships with Maghreb states to expand their spheres of influence. Moreover, these new partnerships provide strategic benefits in what these governments view as long-term regional conflicts in which the United States is either indifferent or preoccupied with different objectives.

External actors are more willing than ever to expend significant political and financial capital to influence political outcomes in the Maghreb.

Turkey has sought a greater role in Arab affairs and opportunities to promote the Justice and Development Party (AKP)'s model of governance. Its efforts have often overlapped with those of Qatar, which supports Islamist movements as a tool for greater regional influence. The UAE, often in cooperation with Egyptian President Abdel Fattah al-Sisi, has supported status quo forces, including anti-Islamist political factions in Tunisia and Libya, while deepening its partnership with Morocco. Saudi Arabia and the UAE fear that if countries in the Maghreb develop transparent and representative politics or if political Islamists lead governments, it could stoke political opposition in the Gulf, undermining their own authority. Growing insecurity and radicalism fueled by jihad in Syria and the security vacuum in Libya also affect every country in the region. For governments in the Gulf Cooperation Council (GCC), Egypt, and Turkey, these trends are not merely foreign policy issues, but directly impact their own domestic politics.

Given the stakes, these external actors are more willing to act independently and expend significant political and financial capital to influence political outcomes in the Maghreb. For the United States, the Maghreb is also increasingly important. But unlike GCC governments and Turkey, which are working to reshape regional alliances for strategic purposes, the United States is less concerned with specific political outcomes in individual Maghreb countries than with a status quo that promotes security, government capacity to provide basic needs for citizens, and economic growth. The problem, for the United States and the region, is that the policies of other actors, including U.S. allies, often do more to prolong conflicts than to support political compromise and power-sharing in the Maghreb. These political divisions and conflicts create a vacuum exploited by radical groups, undermine state capacity to provide for citizens, and prevent consensus for urgently needed economic and political reforms.

THE NEW MAGHREB LANDSCAPE

In the past, Maghreb dynamics were relatively contained within the region. For most of the last half century, the Maghreb looked toward Europe, which had the most at stake in the region. The European Union launched the European Neighborhood Policy (ENP) in 2004 partly to insulate the continent from the Maghreb's challenges. The EU and its member states provided the vast majority of the Maghreb's foreign aid, foreign direct investment (FDI), and trade. European governments poured billions of euros into promoting political and economic reform intended to improve conditions to the south, and (thereby) lower incentives for migration north. Algeria and Libya provided an important source of energy. And millions of North Africans settled in Europe, mostly seeking better job prospects. Algeria's war against Islamist groups in the 1990s sparked isolated attacks in France but did not pose a strategic threat. Politics remained local, and European partners largely provided aid and support to promote stability rather than regime change to oust autocratic leaders.[2]

The Sunni Arab Gulf states, by contrast, largely left the Maghreb alone. Deep ties existed between Morocco and Gulf monarchies, but personal relationships, rather than overlapping interests, were paramount. Gulf Arab governments' policy priorities focused on challenges closer to home such as wars in Iraq and Afghanistan, turmoil in Yemen, and the rise of Shi'ite Iran. The Maghreb was a part of the Arab world, but it was not essential to the GCC states.

In a short period of time, however, the Maghreb changed. Some change has been revolutionary while some has been planned and evolutionary. In every case, the outcome of political struggles and the decisions of governments not only will shape individual countries in the Maghreb but also will have widespread consequences for a range of actors in the Middle East and North Africa. Leaders and societies face a number of critical choices in the future. The choices include how states respond to radicalism and violent extremism, how to solve Libya's crisis, whether to make painful economic reforms, and how to manage popular demands for more transparent government and economic opportunities. The outcomes of these trends will be felt far beyond the Maghreb's borders.

Tunisia

Of all the Maghreb countries, Tunisia has witnessed the most change and holds the most promise of creating a new political system based on representative government and consensus. Ennahda's decision in late 2013 to relinquish power was

2. In 2011 the French and British governments supported military action to overthrow the Qaddafi regime.

partially influenced by the military coup in Egypt, which ousted President Mohammed Morsi and the Muslim Brotherhood in July 2013, and declining popularity due to rising terrorist violence. Still, given Tunisia's past authoritarianism and repression of political Islamists, it was a bold move that likely saved the country from deeper polarization and political violence.

Since then, Tunisia has made historic strides forward, with another round of free and transparent parliamentary and presidential elections. Yet the lack of political and economic vision in the new government further raises doubts about whether it can make structural reforms that move Tunisia beyond its pre-revolutionary socioeconomic status quo.

Tunisia's greatest hurdle moving forward may be how to dismantle an economic system built to support authoritarianism.

Several looming challenges make Tunisia's path uncertain. Tunisia's greatest hurdle moving forward may be how to dismantle an economic system built to support authoritarianism in favor of a system that is more inclusive and spurs trade, economic growth, and job creation. Political uncertainty has hurt tourism, formerly more than seven percent of gross domestic product (GDP),[3] and European economic woes, combined with perceived political instability and labor unrest in Tunisia, have hurt foreign investment and exports to Europe, Tunisia's largest trading partner. But structural problems also undermine Tunisia's economic performance. According to the World Bank, more than half of Tunisia's economy remains closed or is subject to entry restrictions, while low productivity, lingering corruption, and inefficiencies continue.[4] Monopolies and import laws intended to reward supporters of the Ben Ali regime remain in place, creating price distortions, informal economic activity, and lost tax revenue.[5] The combined impact not only affects consumers but also creates an unattractive climate for investment and entrepreneurship.

Tackling many of these economic problems requires political decisions that could hurt entrenched business interests, many of which support the new government. It also means considering the interests of Tunisia's powerful labor unions, most importantly the Union Générale Tu-

3. International Monetary Fund, *Tunisia: Selected Issues* (Country Report 10/109), May 2010, 2, https://www.imf.org/external/pubs/ft/scr/2010/cr10109.pdf.
4. The World Bank, "Tunisia: Development Policy Review," May 24, 2014, 82, http://www-wds.worldbank.org/external/default/WDSContentServer/WDSP/IB/2014/09/16/000456286_20140916144712/Rendered/PDF/861790DPROP12800Box385314B00PUBLIC0.pdf.
5. *The Unfinished Revolution: Bringing Opportunity, Good Jobs and Greater Wealth to all Tunisians*, The World Bank, May 24, 2014, http://www-wds.worldbank.org/external/default/WDSContentServer/WDSP/IB/2014/09/16/000456286_20140916144712/Rendered/PDF/861790DPR0P12800Box385314B00PUBLIC0.pdf.

nisienne du Travail (UGTT) and the Union Tunisienne de l'Industrie, du Commerce et de l'Artisanat (UTICA), which together have the power to mobilize tens of thousands of members. The unions don't necessarily oppose structural reforms, though the UGTT has called for public sector salary increases and opposed loosening labor protections. Most importantly, they seek to ensure that any reforms are balanced with policies that help the middle class. The new government faces not only economic policy dilemmas but also the need to manage citizens' expectations about how quickly it can improve their lives and its ability to steer the country forward.

The backdrop of growing insecurity in Tunisia and in the region makes Tunisia's tasks much harder and creates a heightened threat environment. The March 18 attack on the Bardo Museum, which killed more than 20 people, is a stark reminder that Tunisia remains at the intersection of several radical currents including homegrown militants, al Qaeda, the Islamic State group (ISG), and various groups fighting jihad in Syria. According to Tunisian officials, between 2,400 and 3,000 Tunisians have traveled to fight in Syria since the uprising began in 2011, making Tunisians one of the largest foreign national groups fighting in Syria. Many of those joined the al Qaeda-affiliated Jabhat al Nusra and later the ISG. An insurgency still rages on Tunisia's western border, where the Okba ibn Nafaa Brigade, affiliated with al Qaeda in the Islamic Maghreb (AQIM), has killed dozens of Tunisian security forces since 2012.[6] Meanwhile, violence and instability in Libya heighten security risks in Tunisia.

Greater political coordination between the government, military, and interior ministry in late 2013 helped enable Tunisia's security forces to launch a more cohesive counterterrorism push on several fronts. In 2014 alone, security forces arrested more than 1,500 suspected militants, though how many are actually involved in militant activity is unclear. The danger, however, is that a strategy that relies too heavily on security or is seen as violating human rights could trigger a backlash and greater sympathy for jihadi-salafists and create a new wave of radicalization.

Libya

How to end Libya's multiple conflicts, most importantly the polarizing fight between two rival governments, is one of the Maghreb's biggest challenges. These conflicts boil down to a question of legitimacy—a battle over who has the legitimacy to head Libya's central government and begin the long process of rebuilding the country, which was left with few functioning institutions after four decades of Muammar el-

---

6. According to some reports the Okba ibn Nafaa Brigade has pledged allegiance to ISG Caliph Abu Omar al-Baghdadi. What is more likely is that a faction of the group has pledged allegiance to the ISG while part remains affiliated with AQIM in Algeria.

Qaddafi's rule. Those who fought Qaddafi claim revolutionary legitimacy. Some claim legitimacy from elections. Hundreds of militias claim legitimacy by force of arms or tribal affiliation. In the short period since Qaddafi's fall in October 2011, Libya has had three governing bodies: the National Transitional Council (NTC), which formed during the rebellion against Qaddafi; the General National Congress (GNC), which was elected in July 2012; and the Council of Deputies (House of Representatives), elected in June 2014. It has had six prime ministers, most of whom quit or were forced out by armed militias.

Many Libyans who worked for a negotiated solution to Libya's conflicts view General Heftar's forces as simply one more militia among many.

Throughout most of 2014, competing factions contested the legitimacy of elections, political officials, and government decisions through intimidation and violence. The result was intense fighting for control, which created two competing governments.

Libya Dawn, a loose coalition of Islamists and numerous militias affiliated with Misratan tribal forces, controls Tripoli. The coalition includes the Muslim Brotherhood-inspired Justice and Construction Party (JCP) and members of the Libyan Islamic Fighting Group (LIFG), which once fought alongside al Qaeda in Afghanistan and is designated by the United States as a foreign terrorist organization.

The Tobruk-based government, the House of Representatives, allied itself with General Khalifa Heftar, a former Qaddafi officer who spent years of exile in the United States and was at one point funded by the CIA to overthrow Qaddafi.[7] Heftar calls for eradicating all Islamists, including those that have participated in parliamentary elections, and in May 2014 launched air and ground attacks against Islamist forces in the Eastern city of Benghazi. He has been accused of using cluster munitions in civilian areas. Many Libyans who worked for a negotiated solution to Libya's conflicts view General Heftar's forces as simply one more militia among many.

It is tempting to boil Libya's conflict down to a battle between Islamist and nationalist forces. But the reality is more complicated. The country is divided along multiple fault lines, which fuel conflict beyond the Tripoli-Tobruk clash and include tribal, ethnic, and regional feuds. In the southern city of Sabha, for example, clashes between different tribal factions have killed hundreds of people since 2012.[8]

7. Heftar called his force the Libyan National Army and allied himself with forces in Libya's regular army, including air force units stationed in the East. For a profile of Heftar see Jon Lee Anderson, "The Unravelling," *New Yorker*, February 23, 2015, http://www.newyorker.com/magazine/2015/02/23/unravelling.
8. "Libya's south scarred by tribal battles," *Al Jazeera*, January 24, 2014, http://www.aljazeera.com/news/africa/2014/01/libya-south-scarred-tribal-battles-201412461116244625.html.

Political deadlock between competing governments, meanwhile, has allowed the spread of radical militants, including those allied with the ISG. The ISG sees an opportunity to create a foothold in Libya, which it could use to expand throughout the Maghreb and Sahel. For the moment, the ISG is strongest in Derna, a coastal town of about 100,000 people, but it has branches in Fezzan and Tripolitania as well. It is increasing its operations in Sirte and Benghazi, where it is trying to co-opt Ansar al Shari'a fighters and other jihadi-salafists, and Tripoli, where it reportedly launched the attack against the Corinthia Hotel in January 2015. That attack killed 10 people, including an American security contractor.[9] It is unclear whether Libya Dawn's approach to jihadi-salafists might shift after the Corinthia attack, leading to a military showdown at some point in the future. Should the ISG forces expand, they could also trigger a more direct clash with Misratan and other tribal militias who may not appreciate the radical group's encroachment. What is clear is that without future cooperation between the Tripoli and Tobruk governments, it will be difficult to root out the ISG and other jihadi-salafists.

In the meantime, political deadlock and insecurity threaten Libya's primary source of hard currency: energy. Hydrocarbons account for nearly 96 percent of total government revenue and 98 percent of export revenue.[10] Production cuts due to violence and blockades of oil ports have caused a significant drop in production and export. Production at its low point dipped to fewer than 250,000 barrels per day (bpd) in April 2014 and hovered around 333,000 bpd for most of 2014. That is still well below the 1.6 million bpd Libya pumped during Qaddafi's rule. Over the long term, the unreliability of Libyan oil exports, the current global oversupply, and price pressures could hinder a future government's efforts to build a legitimate and functioning state system that provides security and basic services to its citizens. Without substantial oil revenue, Libya will be dependent on external aid.

Libya's conflict threatens all of its neighbors. After decades of meddling in others' internal affairs, Libya has become an arena for proxy battles by external actors. While foreign governments seek to shape political outcomes, local factions are manipulating outside political and financial support for their own agendas. This mix creates a dangerous cycle and makes establishing a legitimate government in control of Libya's territory, security, and resources a daunting challenge, which could take years, if it is even possible.

---

9. Daniela Deane and Adam Goldman, "American among victims of attack on hotel in Libyan capital," *Washington Post*, January 27, 2015, http://www.washingtonpost.com/world/gunmen-storm-tripoli-luxury-hotel/2015/01/27/ae26ec1e-a611-11e4-a06b-9df2002b86a0_story.html.
10. Crude oil accounts for 79 percent of hydrocarbon exports. See U.S. Energy Information Administration, "Libya," November 25, 2014, http://www.eia.gov/countries/cab.cfm?fips=LY.

Algeria

Algeria has enjoyed a rare decade of political predictability and relative security after years of violence and terrorism. The future, however, will be complicated. Algeria is largely surrounded by insecure borders and weak governments in Mali, Tunisia, Niger, and Libya while its western border with Morocco remains shut because of diplomatic conflict. The global price of oil plummeted by nearly half in 2014, and oil contributes approximately 95 percent of export revenues and 60 percent of the state budget.[11] On the political front, 78-year-old President Abdelaziz Bouteflika, who ushered in more than a decade of relative calm, does not have a clear successor.[12] Other senior regime figures are also aging or ill, raising the specter for some Algerians of an unmanaged, and potentially violent, generational transition.

Rising energy prices over the last two decades enabled the government to unite its own disparate factions around a shared source of income, pay off the country's external debt, boost foreign currency reserves, fund patronage networks, and buy off former militants as part of a national reconciliation process. Over the last several years, the government could respond to thousands of demonstrations and protests and placate the public by addressing a range of socioeconomic demands, from housing to jobs.

The recent drop in oil revenue already is having an impact, as Algeria is expecting a budget shortfall of more than $50 billion in 2015.[13] Algeria has the world's fifteenth largest foreign exchange reserves, and government savings will reportedly cover the vast majority (88.3 percent) of the projected deficit.[14] Lower government revenue that leads to cuts in spending will not necessarily trigger mass protests. But it makes the government's stabilization policy harder during a tumultuous period across the region. Public demonstrations have failed to translate into structural political changes, but the specter of the oil price collapse in the 1980s and its political reverberations still weigh heavily on Algerian policymakers. In 1986 the price of oil dropped to $10 per barrel, forcing the government to slash its public spending over the next few years. Economic crisis combined with a series of clashes between protestors and the army in 1988 contributed to the regime's decision to hold open elections, which political Islamists won. In 1991, the army stepped in and canceled the election results. A decade-long battle between the government and Islamists left approximately 150,000 people dead

11. International Monetary Fund, "Algeria: Selected Issues (Country Report 14/34)," February 2014, 26, http://www.imf.org/external/pubs/ft/scr/2014/cr1434.pdf.

12. According to the Algerian constitution, should the president die in office or become incapacitated, the president of the upper chamber of parliament becomes interim president, followed by presidential elections 60 days later.

13. The budget law envisions revenues of 46.9 billion euros and outlays of 88.6 billion euros, an increase of 15.7 percent this year, for a deficit equivalent to 22.1 percent of GDP. "Algeria sees 42 bn euro budget deficit on weaker oil," Agence France-Presse, December 30, 2014, http://www.dailymail.co.uk/wires/afp/article-2891635/Algeria-sees-42-bn-euro-budget-deficit-weaker-oil.html.

14. Ibid.

and the country traumatized. President Abdelaziz Bouteflika's rule ushered in greater stability, and high hydrocarbon prices made it possible.

Lower prices, however, aren't the only problem. Algeria's overall oil and gas production is declining.

Lower prices, however, aren't the only problem. Algeria's overall oil and gas production is declining. Since 2006, lower production, stagnant reserves, and higher domestic consumption have meant less oil and gas for export.[15] To shore up its declining revenues and falling production in mature fields, Algeria has launched an ambitious strategy to produce shale gas, including by investing $70 billion over the next 20 years.[16] Organized protests by local communities and environmental groups against developing shale in southern Algeria, however, have created a new hurdle for the government. The prime minister has promised to delay shale development for several years. Yet the centrality of energy production to government spending means that it will likely move forward despite domestic opposition.

While Algeria's domestic policy remains relatively constant, its regional policy has shifted in subtle yet significant ways. It has a longstanding policy of non-interference in neighbors' affairs and opposing foreign military intervention in the region.[17] But after Algeria opposed French military intervention in Mali, France claimed that Algeria had granted it overflight rights in support of Operation Serval in January 2013 to evict Islamist militants from Mali. Then Algeria reportedly cooperated closely with Tunisian security forces in fighting militants on the Tunisian-Algerian border. Algeria also has worked more closely with Egypt to find a solution to Libya's security vacuum, although its stance on a parallel track of negotiations taking place in Morocco is unclear. In a continuation of its efforts to lead a non-Western response to instability in the Sahel over the past decade, Algeria has mediated Mali's peace talks and sought to lead a forum of Saharan countries fighting terrorism. But internal debate over intervention persists at the highest levels of government.

---

15. U.S. Energy Information Administration, "Algeria," July 24, 2014, http://www.eia.gov/countries/cab.cfm?fips=ag.

16. Besides six shale gas basins that Sonatrach has already listed in the Sahara desert, drilling operations are about to start offshore for the first time. "Algeria looks to invest $70 bln in shale gas over 20 years," Agence France-Presse, January 11, 2015, http://english.alarabiya.net/en/business/energy/2015/01/11/Algeria-looks-to-invest-70-bln-in-shale-gas-over-20-years-.html.

17. Algeria has repeatedly opposed requests for military intervention in Mali and Libya. "Algeria rules out military intervention in Mali," *Al Monitor*, June 16, 2014, http://www.al-monitor.com/pulse/security/2014/06/algeria-mali-will-not-intervene.html#.

There are also internal debates over how openly and closely to cooperate with the United States, though ties have deepened considerably under Bouteflika.

Algeria's ruling oligarchy understands that the country and the region are changing. New and old challenges create uncertainty about the future. Yet how to address those changes and challenges divides Algeria's power centers. The regime seeks to create sufficient openings to minimally satisfy popular demands while maintaining as much of the current balance of power as possible. This will require both political and economic incentives and opportunities to cooperate. Should cooperation break down, it will likely further paralyze decisionmaking on critical issues such as energy licensing, foreign investment, and political participation. As a large and influential country, Algeria's decisions on all of these issues will reverberate throughout the Maghreb and beyond.

Morocco

Morocco successfully escaped the political instability that affected its North African neighbors in 2011 by responding swiftly to popular uprisings. Less than a month after youth protests erupted in February 2011, King Mohammed VI launched a series of political reforms granting enhanced parliamentary powers through a new constitution. Later that year Morocco held parliamentary elections won by the Justice and Development Party (PJD), an Islamist political party that has competed in parliamentary politics for more than a decade. Yet rather than addressing Morocco's socioeconomic challenges and demands for greater transparency and economic equality, the reforms reinforced the palace's control of nearly every aspect of Morocco's political, economic, religious, and security affairs. The palace-driven reforms effectively split the opposition by offering limited concessions that satisfied some but not others. Further, by allowing the PJD to head the government for the first time, the king neutralized the most organized political party that might oppose him. Through its electoral victory, the PJD went from being the loyal opposition to the king's chief defender, creating a mutually dependent relationship between the PJD and the palace.

Though there is no serious call for revolutionary change at the moment, challenges loom on several fronts that could disrupt Morocco's political stability. One is the uncertain future of the Al Adl Wa'l Ihsane (Justice and Charity) movement, a tolerated Islamist group that rejects the king's religious and political rule and is thus barred from parliamentary and municipal politics. If the movement requests to form a political party at some point in the future, it could disrupt parliament's acquiescence to the monarchy's executive powers and force a greater debate on the balance of power between king and parliament. Even absent an entry into formal politics, the group has a vibrant youth wing that is likely to play an important role in any future grassroots opposition.[18]

18. Justice and Charity's youth wing initially cooperated with the February 20 Movement in 2011, though it later withdrew its support.

The second challenge is tackling a long list of socioeconomic problems. Morocco's widely publicized reforms and impressive economic growth over the last few years have largely benefited the ruling elite while failing to address widespread calls to fight corruption and create greater transparency, economic opportunity, and equality. Many of these problems are deeply entrenched in Morocco's power structure and elite patronage systems. Without addressing the deeper issues of economic inequality and opportunity, however, criticism of the king and his power circle known as the *makhzen* is likely to continue, posing political challenges and greater scrutiny of the king's executive authority.[19]

Third, Morocco faces the common regional challenge of growing radicalization, which has lured an estimated 1,500 to 2,000 Moroccan fighters to jihad in Syria since 2011. Most originally joined Jabhat al Nusra's Moroccan led battalions, though many defected to the ISG beginning in 2014. Moroccan security services have reportedly arrested dozens of local cells they claim were either affiliated with AQIM or the ISG, planning attacks, or sending Moroccans to fight in Syria.[20] The issue is not new. Morocco has battled local jihadi-salafi cells in the past, and dozens of Moroccans fought with al Qaeda during the U.S.-led war in Iraq, though the numbers of Moroccan fighters today far exceed those during the U.S.-led Iraq war.[21]

Morocco has responded to growing radicalization with a program to promote a Moroccan Islamic narrative and identity based on the centrality of the king and the Maliki school of jurisprudence.[22] The objective is to socialize Moroccans to respect state religious ulema (religious scholars) and by extension royal authority. One of the key challenges is creating religious leaders and institutions that resonate with young people and provide a compelling alternative to the radical and rebellious

---

19. Growing criticism and scrutiny of the king's executive powers and wealth has led to a crackdown on dissent and freedom of speech. Criticizing the king remains a criminal offense, though artists and journalists continue pushing the limits of this restriction. Moroccan authorities respond by using the justice system to prosecute public criticism often on trumped up charges, which usually draws more attention. In one high-profile case, a 28-year-old rapper known as "Al-Haqed" (the enraged one) has been a frequent target of the authorities for his songs which have criticized the police and indirectly criticized the king. In one song the activist substituted the word "freedom" for "the king" in a national saying "God, the nation, and the king." See "Rapper Convicted After Apparently Unfair Trial," Human Rights Watch, July 2, 2014, http://www.hrw.org/news/2014/07/02/morocco-rapper-convicted-after-apparently-unfair-trial.
20. Aziz El Yaakoubi, "Moroccan government proposes penalties for nationals fighting in Syria, Iraq," Reuters, September 18, 2014, http://www.reuters.com/article/2014/09/18/us-morocco-security-law-idUSKBN0HD2JU20140918.
21. Craig Whitlock, "Terrorist Networks Lure Young Moroccans to War in Far-Off Iraq," *Washington Post*, February 20, 2007, http://www.washingtonpost.com/wp-dyn/content/article/2007/02/19/AR2007021901168.html.
22. Haim Malka, "The Struggle for Religious Identity in Tunisia and the Maghreb," CSIS, May 2, 2014, http://csis.org/files/publication/140502_Malka_Maghreb_Religious_Identity_Web.pdf.

message of jihadi-salafists. Morocco's efforts are the most comprehensive, but similar strategies are underway in Tunisia, Egypt, and the UAE. This component of what the U.S. government calls countering violent extremism (CVE) is one of the most important government strategies to fight radicalism, and it is a generational struggle. Every country in the region and European countries with sizeable Muslim populations will be affected by Morocco's success or failure and will closely watch its development.

For the GCC countries and Turkey, the Maghreb has become a primary arena for a proxy battle between Islamist and non-Islamist political forces.

PROXY BATTLES AND EXTERNAL INTERVENTION

External actors have watched these developments closely for how they affect their own interests. For the GCC countries and Turkey, the Maghreb has become a primary arena for a proxy battle between Islamist and non-Islamist political forces, and each has steered investments and aid to shore up its allies. Maghreb governments and political forces have played into this dynamic as well, seeing opportunities for aid and external support to further local agendas. GCC states in particular provide financial aid with fewer conditions and no transparency, making them important financial backers for some Maghreb governments and political parties.[23] Results have been mixed. In some cases external support has provided badly needed funds for governments to get through difficult periods, as in the case of Tunisia. In other cases, it deepens already polarized politics, which fuels ongoing conflict, as in Libya.

Regional Players

Since the Arab uprisings began, Qatar and Turkey have supported political Islamists across the Middle East and North Africa. Turkey's ruling AKP shares affinity with political Islamists, and Qatar has supported both Muslim Brotherhood inspired parties and salafi groups.[24] The UAE and Saudi Arabia, in contrast, declared the Muslim Brotherhood a terrorist organization and support nationalist or anti-revolutionary forces throughout the region. For all of these countries, supporting or fighting political Islamists is not merely a foreign policy preference, but is deeply tied to domestic political calculations. For Qatar, Islamists of various stripes have become a useful foreign policy tool.

---

23. For a detailed overview of GCC engagement in the Maghreb see Carolyn Barnett, "GCC-Maghreb Relations in a Changing Regional Order," CSIS, August 2013, http://csis.org/files/publication/130814_Barnett_GCCMaghreb_Web_2.pdf.

24. A number of political Islamist parties operate in the Maghreb including Morocco's PJD, Tunisia's Ennahda, Algeria's Movement for a Peaceful Society (MSP), and Libya's Justice and Construction Party. They may have been inspired by Egypt's Muslim Brotherhood and have sympathy for the broader movement, but none have any open affiliation with Egypt's Muslim Brotherhood, nor do they share a political platform with it.

In Turkey, a victory for political Islamists would enable the AKP to claim that its model is succeeding and give it greater influence in Arab affairs. For Saudi Arabia and the UAE, both of which face domestic Islamist opposition, Muslim Brotherhood victories could inspire greater political opposition at home.

Libya and Tunisia have been the primary battlegrounds within the Maghreb between these competing visions. Both the UAE and Qatar participated in the coalition to defeat Qaddafi in 2011, but they backed different factions during the military campaign and in the aftermath. Now Qatar and Turkey support Libya Dawn, which seized the capital in August 2014 and expelled the elected House of Representatives.[25] The UAE, Saudi Arabia, and Egypt support the Tobruk-based government of Abdullah al-Thinni and military commander Heftar. Their objectives are clear: ensure that Libya doesn't undermine security and the political status quo in neighboring Egypt, and prevent Islamists from controlling Libya.

Gulf intervention did not create the divide in Libya, but strong support for rival governments in Tripoli and Tobruk has triggered more violence and deepened the country's fragmentation. General Heftar vowed to rid Libya of all Islamists, and violence surged after he launched his "Campaign Dignity" with support from the UAE. In an unprecedented move, UAE air force jets bombed Islamist forces aligned with Libya Dawn in Tripoli in August 2014 without informing the U.S. government.[26] Emirati commentators quoted in the press suggested that the UAE was prompted to act to protect its interests because of U.S. inaction in conflicts in Syria and Libya.[27] With foreign backers, rival governments have entrenched their positions and intensified fighting for Libya's oil assets, thereby undermining a UN-led process aimed at reaching a power-sharing agreement.

The United States, in contrast, worked with both the GNC and the House of Representatives when each headed Libya's government. Though it officially recognizes the Tobruk-based government, it has so far publicly refused to supply it with weapons, in part because of discomfort with General Heftar's tactics. Instead, the U.S. government supports the UN-led reconciliation process as the only option to stabilize Libya. In July 2014, the United States shuttered its embassy in Tripoli and evacuated its staff. Though Libya's predicament has an impact on other U.S. allies

---

25. David D. Kirkpatrick and Eric Schmitt, "Arab Nations Strike in Libya, Surprising U.S.," *New York Times*, August 25, 2014, http://www.nytimes.com/2014/08/26/world/africa/egypt-and-united-arab-emirates-said-to-have-secretly-carried-out-libya-airstrikes.html.

26. Ibid.

27. Emirati academic Abdulkhaleq Abdulla for example was quoted by Reuters regarding the airstrikes: "In the light of U.S. inaction in Syria, the message is clear, that you have to take care of your own concerns." See William MacLean, "Libyan raids herald bolder Arab action as U.S. wavers," Reuters, August 26, 2014, http://www.reuters.com/article/2014/08/26/us-libya-security-gulf-idUSKBN0GQ23220140826.

in the region, U.S. policy objectives have remained modest, in part because of the lack of good options and the investment in resources and manpower required to help resolve Libya's multiple conflicts. Moreover, the murder of Ambassador Christopher Stevens and three other Americans has distorted any rational political debate on Libya and lowered the U.S. government's risk tolerance for operating there. Whether the United States has the ability to influence political outcomes in Libya is unclear. Yet, with no formal diplomatic presence, the United States is sitting on the sidelines, while other actors attempt to shape Libya's future.

Beyond Libya, external actors also see much at stake in Tunisia's political transition. Despite overt political support for different political factions from GCC governments and Turkey, Tunisia's main political parties chose political compromise rather than conflict. Unlike Libya, Tunisia has functioning institutions, including the military and police as well political parties, trade unions, and numerous civil society organizations, but the country was not immune to external intervention.

Qatar provided early support for Tunisia's Ennahda-led government and saw an opportunity for political Islamists to lead the country. It backed up its political support with financial assistance, loans, and investments.[28] In 2012 alone, Qatar pledged multiple loans totaling more than $1.5 billion.[29] Following the overthrow of Ben Ali, Qatar's Emir Sheikh Hamad Bin Khalifa al-Thani visited Tunisia and proclaimed that "your martyrs and wounded are also ours."[30] Ennahda leader Rached Ghannouchi's first overseas visit after constituent assembly elections in October 2011 was to Qatar. Qatar provided early support for Tunisia's government at a time when other GCC governments kept Ennahda at a distance.[31] The UAE provided some humanitarian support for Tunisia beginning in 2011 and received Ennahda-affiliated government officials.[32] Still, the UAE had a clear preference for its secularist rival Nidaa Tounes once that party coalesced.[33]

---

28. In 2011 Qatar purchased a 75 percent stake in telephone operation Tunisiana and 99 percent share in Tunisian Qatari Bank. Qatar already owned a stake in Tunisiana through its 51 percent share of Kuwait's Wataniya which controlled 50 percent of Tunisiana. "Qatar Telecom says to boost stake in Tunisiana," Reuters, June 15, 2011, http://www.reuters.com/article/2011/06/15/qtel-tunisiana-idUSLDE75E0M620110615; "Qatar's QNB buys further 49.96 pct in Tunisian Qatari Bank," Reuters, January 23, 2013, http://www.reuters.com/article/2013/01/23/us-qatar-qnb-tunisia-idUSBRE90M0OR20130123.
29. Qatar purchased millions in Tunisian bonds, and invested and supported numerous social and economic projects, though a publicized plan for building a $2 billion oil refinery (which had originally been signed under Ben Ali in 2007) has not materialized. Domestic criticism for the repayment of loan terms created a backlash against Qatar.
30. "Qatar's influence in Tunisia," *Tunis Times*, October 15, 2013, http://www.thetunistimes.com/2013/10/qatars-influence-in-tunisia-91527/.
31. Interim Prime Minister Béji Caïd Essebsi met the Emir of Qatar in April 2011.
32. Ola Salem, "UAE Sends Help for the 'New Tunisia'," *National*, May 4, 2012, http://www.thenational.ae/news/uae-news/uae-sends-help-for-the-new-tunisia.
33. Since Ennahda's resignation from office the UAE has stepped up its support for Nidaa Tounes, which was formed to challenge Ennahda. Prior to the 2014 parliamentary elections, the UAE reportedly donated two armored cars to provide security for Nidaa leader Essebsi and also reportedly flew him on a private jet to visit the country in May 2014, in violation of a 2011 law which prohibits foreign funding for political parties. Mary Atkinson, "'Luxury' cars and a foreign funding scandal in Tunisia," *Middle East Eye*, August 13, 2014, http://www.middleeasteye.net/news/luxury-cars-and-foreign-funding-scandal-tunisia-1891049441.

The UAE recalled its ambassador to Tunisia in September 2013 after President Moncef Marzouki criticized the ousting of President Mohammed Morsi and the Muslim Brotherhood in Egypt.

By contrast, the United States has provided Tunisia with slightly more than $600 million since 2011.[34] The sum is significant by historical standards of U.S. aid to Tunisia, but it is a fraction of what Qatar provided in a single year. It is also a fraction of what the United States spends on some other Middle Eastern countries. Jordan, for example, received $660 million annually between FY2010-2014 as part of a five-year aid package.[35] That number is about to increase with a new aid package that will provide more than $1 billion a year to Jordan.[36]

GCC governments also took great interest in Morocco, a fellow Sunni Arab monarchy. Morocco's longstanding relations with Sunni Arab monarchies in the Gulf have deepened since the Arab uprisings. What the Gulf countries seek is relatively straightforward: to support a fellow monarchy, prevent the spread of political Islamism, and take advantage of investment opportunities where available.

Following the uprisings, Saudi Arabia, the UAE, and Kuwait announced a $2.5 billion aid package for Morocco, and a $285 million loan for Morocco from the Islamic Development Bank.[37] Moreover, the GCC proposed in 2011 that Morocco (and Jordan) join the Council. Though movement toward formal membership has not progressed, the GCC reportedly invited Morocco and Jordan to join a military alliance in March 2014. The proposed alliance would involve Moroccan troops shoring up GCC military forces in exchange for aid.[38] Moroccan military forces have a long history of cooperation with GCC militaries and already station troops in some countries for specified ongoing missions.[39] More recently the UAE and Morocco signed a military cooperation agreement which includes UAE command of Moroccan F-16s participating in the anti-ISG coalition in Syria.

Despite this closeness, Morocco walks a fine line with the GCC and attempts to maintain independent policies. Rather than sharing the UAE's and Saudi Arabia's

---

34. Alexis Arieff and Carla E. Humud, "Political Transition in Tunisia," Congressional Research Service, October 22, 2014, https://www.fas.org/sgp/crs/row/RS21666.pdf.
35. Jeremy Sharp, "Jordan: Background and U.S. Relations," Congressional Research Service, December 2, 2014, http://fpc.state.gov/documents/organization/234976.pdf.
36. "U.S. plans to boost aid to Jordan to $1 billion per year," Reuters, February 3, 2015, http://www.reuters.com/article/2015/02/03/us-jordan-aid-idUSKBN0L72ET20150203.
37. The aid was part of a $5 billion pledge for Morocco and Jordan.
38. Awad Mustafa, "GCC Seeks to Form Military Bloc with Jordan, Morocco," *Defense News*, April 14, 2014, http://www.defensenews.com/article/20140414/DEFREG04/304140018/.
39. Ibid.

opposition to political Islamists, Morocco's king cooperates with the Islamist PJD. At the same time, the monarchy shares the UAE's goal of promoting the Maliki school of Islam as a non-violent alternative to salafi-inspired Islamic teaching and Saudi-style Wahhabism. It also has balanced UAE and Saudi investment with Qatari investment, including a proposed $2.2 billion joint investment fund in Morocco.[40]

Of all the Maghreb countries, Algeria is the most impervious to outside influence and the most vehement in opposing external intervention in the region.

Of all the Maghreb countries, Algeria is the most impervious to outside influence and the most vehement in opposing external intervention in the region. Thus, it approaches GCC activity and other efforts in the Maghreb with suspicion. It has traditionally supported more hawkish pricing policies within OPEC. Algeria opposed the NATO-led military coalition that ousted Qaddafi, warning of dire consequences should Qaddafi be deposed. Algeria, however, has stepped up coordination with its neighbors on Libyan security issues.

France's Assertiveness

European states, most notably the former colonial powers of France, Spain, and Italy, also have direct interests in the Maghreb. Each Maghreb country is a destination for substantial European commercial interests, and Europe hosts sizeable North African immigrant communities that maintain links with their home countries. The Maghreb has for decades provided southern Europe with unskilled labor, and the vast majority of the region's economy is tied to Europe, which is the largest trading partner of each Maghreb state. European imports of Libyan and Algerian energy further bind the two regions.[41] In addition, growing radicalism means that the Maghreb's security is intertwined with that of Europe. Today, European security officials are concerned about radicalized militants moving among North Africa, the jihadi battlefields of Syria, and Europe.

France has pursued an assertive foreign policy in the Maghreb, demonstrating the country's willingness to secure its interests in the region. France was instrumental in building a NATO coalition and persuading the Obama administration to support the effort to oust Qaddafi. Ironically, the toppling of Qaddafi triggered an exodus of Tuareg mercenaries that poured into Mali the following year. A military coup followed, which paved the way for al

40. Souhail Karam, "Gulf states court cash-strapped Morocco with investment," Reuters, November 24, 2011, http://www.reuters.com/article/2011/11/24/qatar-morocco-investment-idUSL5E7MO46120111124.
41. Italy for example, is dependent on Libya for nearly one quarter of its energy imports.

Qaeda-linked militants to seize control of parts of northern Mali in 2012. In response, France launched Operation Serval. It later expanded its deployments to nearly 3,000 troops across Mauritania, Mali, Niger, and Chad through Operation Barkane, which has replaced Serval.[42]

The United States has supported France's military missions in the Sahel, which are also intended to secure the Maghreb, by providing intelligence, surveillance, and reconnaissance support (ISR) as well as heavy lift and transport for French troops and equipment. France continues urging greater international efforts to secure Libya. President François Hollande has so far ruled out unilateral military intervention in Libya. But with forces stationed less than 100 km from Libya's border in Niger, French officials have indicated that French forces would strike militants attempting to cross Libya's border in either direction.[43]

CONSEQUENCES OF U.S. POLICY

U.S. military intervention against Qaddafi as part of a multinational coalition in March 2011 set unrealistically high expectations in the region for greater U.S. action.[44] After the overthrow of Qaddafi, the United States largely left Libya to its own devices. The deterioration of Libya's security situation and the attack on the U.S. consulate in Benghazi dampened U.S. willingness to risk additional lives and resources in a conflict that seemed to have no clear winners.[45] The United States provided greater support for Tunisia's transition following the overthrow of Ben Ali compared to its past support, yet overall support has declined year after year since FY2012 and remains modest compared to aid in other parts of the Middle East.[46]

---

42. More recently French officials have indicated their willingness to deploy more troops in Africa to address the growing threat of Boko Haram in Nigeria. In February 2015 French forces reportedly struck Boko Haram in Northern Nigeria.
43. "France Says Ready to Strike Extremists on Libya Border," Associated Press, January 5, 2015, http://www.nytimes.com/aponline/2015/01/05/world/europe/ap-eu-france-libya.html?_r=0.
44. U.S. military forces also bombed Tripoli in April 1986 after a string of international terrorist incidents supported by the Qaddafi regime. See Bernard Weinraub, "U.S. Jets Hit 'Terrorist Centers' in Libya; Reagan Warns of New Attacks If Needed," *New York Times*, April 15, 1986, http://www.nytimes.com/1986/04/15/politics/15REAG.html.
45. The United States has taken direct action on several occasions, mostly special operations working with the FBI to capture militants wanted in connection with attacks against U.S. citizens. In October 2013 U.S. forces captured Nazih Abdul-Hamed al Ruqai (Abu Anas al-Libi) from the streets of Tripoli, and in June 2014 it captured Ahmed Abu Khattala, a suspected ringleader of the attack on the U.S. compound in Benghazi. U.S. forces also forced the return to port of a rogue shipment of Libyan crude oil in March 2014 to prevent secessionist forces in the east from selling oil outside of government channels. Other covert operations may have occurred without publicity. But for the most part, U.S. policy toward Libya has been minimal compared with the role the United States played in overthrowing Qaddafi. Karen DeYoung, Adam Goldman, and Julie Tate, "U.S. Captured Benghazi Suspect in Secret Raid," *Washington Post*, June 17, 2014, http://www.washingtonpost.com/world/national-security/us-captured-benghazi-suspect-in-secret-raid/2014/06/17/7ef8746e-f5cf-11e3-a3a5-42be35962a52_story.html.
46. Aid in FY15 and FY16 for Tunisia could reverse this trend.

Rather than picking sides in the Maghreb, the United States has engaged with whichever governments are in power, including those led by political Islamists. In the last decade, the United States has built positive relations with every government in the Maghreb,[47] while counterterrorism cooperation, trade, and aid have expanded. But in every case, U.S. actions support incumbent governments rather than shaping politics. The United States has an opportunity to deepen its partnership with Morocco and build new partnerships with Tunisia and Algeria that transcend the narrow issue of counterterrorism. This not only requires greater financial investment, including aid, but a senior-level commitment on both sides to move beyond narrow security interests. The challenge for the United States is that priorities and interests in the Gulf and Levant overshadow the importance of the Maghreb, making the United States a secondary actor in the latter. The consequences of playing a secondary role affect both the United States and the region.

If the U.S. government is less willing to invest in political outcomes, it has to be prepared to accept suboptimal outcomes in some cases.

First, in many cases outside actors with more clearly defined interests are promoting policies that undermine security and in some cases perpetuate conflicts. Libya is the most important example of where a proxy battle encourages competing governments to dig in rather than pursue power-sharing political solutions that could stabilize the country. For the U.S. government, the risk is that its policy defaults to the agenda of its closest allies who are more engaged and invested, but whose interests in some cases diverge from those of the United States. If the U.S. government is less willing to invest in political outcomes, it has to be prepared to accept suboptimal outcomes in some cases. In Libya, for example, a more formal partition of the country is one possible outcome.

Second, the United States runs the risk of being manipulated by Maghreb governments that exaggerate security threats or use U.S. support, training, and equipment to suppress legitimate political opposition. Governments in the region are using the specter of radicalism and ISG expansion to constrain personal freedoms such as freedom of speech. They are increasingly intolerant of criti-

47. Beginning in 2004 the United States and Libya began normalizing relations after decades of hostility. The outbreak of the Libyan uprising and U.S. support for NATO-led military strikes ended cooperation with the Qaddafi regime. Following the overthrow of Qaddafi, the United States recognized Libya's transitional government, the National Transitional Council. It now recognizes the Tobruk-based House of Representatives government.

cism, and some have passed sweeping anti-terrorism laws that apply broad definitions of terrorism that can be easily abused. If U.S. security cooperation, training, and aid are abused and directed against legitimate political opposition, it could deepen anti-American sentiment, potentially threatening the lives of U.S. citizens in the region while fueling greater radicalization.

Third, by not clearly defining policy objectives and interests in the Maghreb, the United States runs the risk of being manipulated by other external actors who seek to enlist U.S. help to further their own policy goals. For example, French government lobbying persuaded the U.S. government to support limited U.S. military action in Libya in March 2011. What started as an air campaign to protect the people of Benghazi turned into a de facto operation to replace Qaddafi, with no clear plan for who or what would take his place. While some in the administration did aim to topple Qaddafi from the outset, there was little public or Congressional debate about the operation's potential ramifications.

Fourth, by overemphasizing security and counterterrorism in the Maghreb, the United States is missing an opportunity to build more lasting partnerships that transcend governments. Trade and investment are important areas to expand, for example. Yet, small domestic markets, language barriers, political risk, and complicated regulatory environments are obstacles to investment by U.S. companies and more difficult to address through U.S. aid programs. The United States can work with governments to improve their economic systems, but ultimately economic reforms require difficult political decisions and commitment by governments and entrenched business interests in the region, which may benefit from maintaining the status quo.

LOOKING AHEAD

Patterns of external support for different political factions and governments in the Maghreb have strengthened alliances in the Middle East and North Africa. Overlapping interests in fighting radicalism, promoting quietist Islam, and strengthening the political status quo have deepened the UAE's engagement in the Maghreb. Qatar and Turkey continue to support political Islamists, though outside of Libya, that mission has lost some momentum. This leaves the U.S. government in the awkward position of trying to balance the competing interests of its allies both in the Maghreb and outside and finding itself distanced from its partners on a number of crucial questions, even as they share a commitment to fighting radicalism and strengthening the status quo in some countries.

While the United States is more active today in the Maghreb than ever before, it is not going to fix the region's problems or invest heavily in political outcomes.

Rather, it is prepared to accept a higher level of insecurity and uncertainty. This approach reflects the constraints and challenges of the United States' broader foreign policy and risk aversion in the Middle East and North Africa as well as its priorities. Though the current dynamics may be manageable, they will not remain static. Allowing other governments to frame the region's issues and determine policy undermines U.S. interests, risks leading to outcomes that perpetuate insecurity in the Maghreb, and in some cases deepens sources of conflict and discontent that sparked the Arab uprisings.

For the moment, the United States sees the Maghreb largely through a security lens. Whether that changes depends on developments both inside and outside the region. Maghreb governments will play a role, but so will the actions of outside actors in the Gulf, Turkey, and Europe. The United States may not prioritize the Maghreb over other foreign policy interests in the Middle East. But setting policy priorities within the region that are broader will make the United States more relevant.

How Maghreb governments play into larger external power struggles will affect their own futures. Rather than seeking to address a range of political and socioeconomic challenges, these new alliances could undermine security, open new wounds, and deepen existing fault lines. As the rapid changes in the region attest, governments and political actors in the region will have to manage these competing interests in an increasingly complex and polarizing environment. ■

8 Egypt in the Region

CAROLYN BARNETT

It wasn't long ago that someone sitting down to relax at the end of the day almost anywhere in the Middle East might turn on a radio to hear an Egyptian singer, turn on the TV to watch an Egyptian soap opera, or catch a film with an Egyptian cinema star. For decades in the last century, too, many Arabs looked to Egypt for political leadership within the region.

But by late 2013, a prominent commentator on Gulf affairs asserted that major cities in the Gulf (in particular Dubai, Abu Dhabi, and Doha) had overtaken the likes of Cairo and Beirut as the symbolic centers of the Arab world.[1] Vigorous debate ensued, and many felt that a city such as Cairo—and a country such as Egypt—could hardly be supplanted.[2]

Since 2011 events have left Egypt's health and future trajectory uncertain. Yet many have continued to argue that Egypt is a bellwether for the Middle East as a whole. When protests jumped in January 2011 from Tunis to Cairo, the region's and the world's attention quickly shifted east as

1. Sultan Sooud Al Qassemi, "Thriving Gulf Cities Emerge as New Centers of Arab World," *Al Monitor*, October 8, 2013, http://www.al-monitor.com/pulse/originals/2013/10/abu-dhabi-dubai-doha-arab-centers.html.
2. See "Hel ihtallat mudun al-Khalij makanat al-mudun al-arabiyya al-'ariqa?" [Have the cities of the Gulf taken the place of the old Arab cities?], *BBC Arabic*, October 9, 2013, http://www.bbc.co.uk/arabic/interactivity/2013/10/131009_comments_new_arabcities_, esp. the comments section; Michael Collins Dunn, "The Debate Over Sultan Sooud Al Qassemi's Article on Gulf Cities," Middle East Institute, October 15, 2013, http://mideasti.blogspot.ae/2013/10/the-debate-over-sultan-sooud-al.html; and Al Qassemi's own round-up of the debate, "Responses to Gulf Cities as new Arab Centres of Culture & Commerce article," *Felix Arabia* (blog), October 15, 2013, http://sultanalqassemi.blogspot.com/2013/10/responses-to-gulf-cities-as-new-arab.html.

well. Judging from the media coverage, it almost seemed that Zine el-Abidine Ben Ali's overthrow had been merely the dress rehearsal for the uprising against Egyptian President Hosni Mubarak. As one Bahraini activist stated that February, "[Egypt is] either the sick man of the Arab world, or it could be the healthy man that could take us to new heights."[3]

Yet the reversal of the historical pattern is striking. Today, rather than Egypt taking a leading role in the region, other powers in the region have been taking a leading role in Egypt. For some, Egypt's trajectory epitomizes the failure of the "Arab Spring" to translate into sustained, democratic, inclusive political processes and institutions. For others—most importantly Saudi Arabia (a former rival to Egypt) and the United Arab Emirates (UAE)—Egypt has become ground zero in the effort to sideline politically ambitious Islamist groups and a central arena in the struggle against violent jihadi-salafi organizations. The overthrow of Mubarak in Egypt introduced uncertainty into the region's politics that Gulf states found troubling. They feared that forces opposed to them could come to power in Egypt and that a successful democracy in Egypt might inspire further demands for democratization elsewhere.

It is unclear whether the Gulf states have a specific positive agenda for Egypt's future. But they do appear to think that economic recovery and growth without political liberalization can serve as a basis for future stability there and elsewhere in the region. And they have shown their willingness to step in to prevent short-term economic failure. They also appear to see Egypt as a focal point for strengthening a renewal of "apolitical Islam" in the region, both through traditional religious institutions such as Al Azhar and through the personality of President Abdel Fattah al-Sisi. From their perspective, it is necessary to reimpose security and stability across the Middle East and promote a version of Islam defined primarily by its political quietism, or at least its rejection of political opposition to sitting rulers. The Gulf states believe this effort must succeed in Egypt if it is to succeed anywhere.

Those at the helm in Egypt, in turn, have sought to wield their country's symbolic power to secure their own stability. Unlike throughout much of the twentieth century, however, the threat and promise Egypt hold out today rest on its vulnerability rather than its power. Instead of procuring aid and assistance by suggesting that Egypt might strengthen alternative alliances or interfere abroad, today Egypt procures aid and assistance by highlighting its internal woes. The message it projects is that Egypt is fighting terrorism and potential economic disaster, and those who care about Egypt's future—and by extension that of the Middle East as a whole—should help it win those fights on its terms.

3. Borzou Daraghi, "Change in Egypt could restore its centrality to Arab world," *Los Angeles Times*, February 4, 2011, http://articles.latimes.com/2011/feb/04/world/la-fg-egypt-arab-world-20110204.

EGYPTIAN STRATEGY AND REGIONAL POWER IN THE TWENTIETH CENTURY

Throughout its modern history, Egypt's rulers have faced a common strategic challenge: calibrating how much autonomy to give up to secure external resources needed for domestic political and economic purposes. European states used usurious lending backed by military might in the nineteenth century to dominate Egypt. Egyptian rulers since then have been wary of coming too much under another power's thumb. Even as it resisted such domination, however, Egypt in the twentieth century remained a prize for outsiders. Egyptian leaders—in particular Gamal Abdel Nasser—used that status as leverage to seek aid from all corners.

Even as it resisted such domination, however, Egypt in the twentieth century remained a prize for outsiders.

During the Cold War, the United States tried to woo Egypt, but with little success. U.S. foreign assistance in the 1950s and 1960s, mostly food aid, was predicated on hopes that this would induce the Egyptians to reject Soviet overtures.[4] But the United States would not supply Nasser with something essential to his domestic positioning: weapons. So he looked elsewhere, signing a $250 million arms deal in 1955 with Czechoslovakia. That drove a rift between Egypt and the United States and kicked off a series of events[5] that culminated in Nasser's decision to nationalize the Suez Canal. U.S. aid fluctuated at modest levels in the years that followed.[6] For a long time, there was little incentive for the United States to try to strengthen its ties with Egypt, and it seemed unlikely that Nasser would find advantage in siding too closely with either the United States or the Soviet Bloc.

The Soviet Union tried harder than the United States to woo Egypt and bring the country into its orbit, but it found Nasser hard to get. The USSR was far more generous to Nasser than the United States ever was, both in the amount of aid granted and the terms on which it was given.[7] The Soviets began providing military aid to

---

4. Jeremy Sharp, "U.S. Foreign Assistance to the Middle East: Historical Background, Recent Trends, and FY2011 Request," Congressional Research Service, June 15, 2010, 22, https://www.fas.org/sgp/crs/mideast/RL32260.pdf.

5. In particular, the United States withdrew its offer of credit to help fund construction of the Aswan High Dam in 1956.

6. U.S. aid dropped from $33.3 million in 1956 to $1 million in 1957. By 1962 it had reached a pre-1967 high of $200.5 million. After the 1967 Arab-Israeli war, the United States cut all aid to Egypt, though some small loans re-materialized by 1972. Jeremy Sharp, "Egypt: Background and U.S. Relations," Congressional Research Service, June 5, 2014, 16, https://www.fas.org/sgp/crs/mideast/RL33003.pdf.

7. According to Waterbury, Egyptian official 'Aziz Sidqi claimed it was favorable terms for aid that drew Egypt closer to the Soviets rather than "socialist affinity." John Waterbury, *The Egypt of Nasser and Sadat: The Political Economy of Two Regimes* (Princeton: Princeton University Press, 1983), 397.

Egypt in 1955 through the Czech arms deal. Despite tensions, the relationship grew: in January 1958 the USSR gave Egypt a $158 million loan and $100 million in aid for the Aswan Dam—more than it had ever granted a non-aligned state.[8] By 1975, estimates suggest that "the total flow of socialist economic and military resources to Egypt" over the preceding 20 years came to $6.8 billion, largely financed by Egyptian debt.[9]

While Nasser sought aid from competing global powers, he remained focused on building Egypt's strength within the region. That meant dealing with two strategic foes: Israel and the conservative Arab states, especially Saudi Arabia and Jordan (considered enemies of Arab unity).[10] Nasser championed Egypt as the protector and savior of the beleaguered Palestinian people, and he fought two wars against Israel in 1956 and 1967. When the latter ended in a crushing defeat, it was the beginning of the end of his political career.[11]

Nasser's rivalry with the Arab monarchies was, in contrast, both a cold war and a proxy war. Nasser stood as the beacon for revolutionary Arab nationalism, socialism, and republicanism: three trends that were anathema to the region's remaining monarchs.[12] For much of the 1960s, Egypt and Saudi Arabia also waged a proxy war in North Yemen, whose leader, Imam al-Badr, was overthrown by republicans in a 1962 coup. By the end of the conflict, Egypt had more than 70,000 troops in Yemen, or nearly half its total army.[13] For Nasser, coming to the Yemeni republicans' aid was in large part a way of demonstrating to a domestic audience the power of his person and ideology. It also demonstrated to the world what Egypt could accomplish. Major domestic development and infrastructure projects—the Aswan Dam being the archetypal undertaking—further underscored the argument for Egyptian greatness and achievement.

Until near the end of Sadat's time in power, this basic pattern held: Egypt stood against Israel and the monarchs and was not aligned with either the United States or Soviet Union.[14]

---

8. Galia Golan, *Soviet Policies in the Middle East From World War II to Gorbachev* (New York: Cambridge University Press, 1990), 54.
9. Waterbury, *The Egypt of Nasser and Sadat*, 398.
10. Anthony Nutting, *Nasser* (New York: EP Dutton & Co., Inc., 1972), 320.
11. Ibid., 425–451.
12. In part due to this rivalry, in the 1950s and 1960s, Saudi Arabia took in and harbored intellectual refugees from Egypt after Nasser's crack down on the Muslim Brotherhood. Ironically, given recent developments discussed below, it was in large part Saudi Arabia's hospitality that made possible the survival, renewal, and flourishing of the Egyptian Muslim Brotherhood. For a detailed discussion of this period and the Brotherhood's integration into Saudi state and society, see Stéphane Lacroix, *Awakening Islam: The Politics of Religious Dissent in Contemporary Saudi Arabia* (Cambridge: Harvard University Press, 2011).
13. Nutting, *Nasser*, 322. Nutting's more detailed chapter on Egypt's involvement in the war is titled, appropriately, "Nasser's Vietnam."
14. Relations with the Soviet Union deteriorated through the 1970s, however; Sadat famously expelled 20,000 Soviet military advisers in 1972, supposedly for withholding military equipment. In 1981, Sadat also expelled Russian diplomats and more than 1,000 Soviet technical advisers, alleging Soviet involvement in inciting sectarian violence between Muslims and Christians. Louise Lief, "Sadat blames Soviet diplomats in Egypt for instigating unrest," *Christian Science Monitor*, September 17, 1981, http://www.csmonitor.com/1981/0917/091750.html.

At the end of the 1970s, Sadat shifted Egypt decisively toward a positive relationship with the United States and away from confrontation with Israel by signing the Camp David Accords. The deal guaranteed Egypt a steady flow of aid and a strategic bond with the United States. Jihadists assassinated Sadat before he could build on the shift he had initiated, but his successor, Mubarak, embraced Egypt's new orientation.

Doing so made Egypt's foreign policy simple compared with what had come before. Egypt grew increasingly close with the United States, the Soviet Union collapsed, and relations between Egypt and Saudi Arabia thawed. Mubarak's transactions were straightforward. He would align with the United States or Saudi Arabia on the issues of greatest concern to them, and they would help promote domestic stability, security, and development in Egypt. Egypt's efforts to get outsiders to support its domestic politics were thus based not on threats of Egyptian action around the region, but on promises of Egyptian political support. But this approach also meant that the government could no longer effectively appeal to national pride or ideology to bolster its legitimacy. Especially as Mubarak's days in power neared their end, he commanded little to none of the popular respect, admiration, or reverence that Nasser or even Sadat had. Egypt's symbolic status at the heart of the Arab world held up thanks to its large population, cultural productivity, and relatively free press.[15] But foreign policy in Egypt had become a liability to those in power rather than an asset.

But foreign policy in Egypt had become a liability to those in power rather than an asset.

AFTER 2011: THE GULF IN EGYPT

On January 25, 2011, demonstrations around Cairo and in other Egyptian cities organized as part of a "Day of Rage"—and set to coincide with the country's Police Day to draw attention to state brutality—ended with the occupation of Tahrir Square. By February 11, Mubarak had stepped down and the Supreme Council of the Armed Forces (SCAF) assumed power. Not long after, Egypt moved toward holding elections for an assembly that would form a committee to write a new constitution.

Leaders and publics across the region looked to events in Egypt as a harbinger of what might happen elsewhere. Power structures across the region seemed as

15. However, especially in the 2000s, others began to chip away at this status. For example, the runaway success of Al Jazeera, based in Qatar, and other channels in the Gulf, Turkey, and Syria challenged Egypt's centrality in Arab television and news media.

though they might collapse. Those who rose up in 2011 and many outside the region saw this as a good thing: the opportunity to reset Middle Eastern politics and put them on a path toward representative government, guarantees for civil liberties and human rights, and inclusive, sustainable economic development. Leaders in the Gulf and in some other parts of the region saw a nightmare unfolding, and not only in terms of potential popular protests and challenges to their rule in the near term.

Leaders in the Gulf and in some other parts of the region saw a nightmare unfolding, and not only in terms of potential popular protests and challenges to their rule in the near term.

The perceived U.S. abandonment of Egypt—or at least of its ally Mubarak—unnerved leaders in the Gulf. In part this was because Washington's actions called into question the reliability of the leaders' own security guarantees from the United States. But it was also because they had come to rely on the United States and assume that it would guarantee Egypt's stability. That assumption was no longer valid. Saudi Arabia, Qatar, the UAE, and other regional actors had had little need to devote resources to Egypt when they believed the United States could (and would) keep Mubarak in power. Without needing to invest much, they would benefit from the Mubarak regime's ability to hold in check the potential threats Egypt could pose to their own security—primarily by exporting political or ideological opposition to Gulf monarchs' rule. The pre-2011 status quo in Egypt was not bad from a Gulf perspective. It would have been nice if Egypt experienced better economic growth and development, but it was not essential. Accompanying this reality was a tacit mutual acceptance among regional leaders against interference in one another's domestic political affairs. That was one reason why the Arab League, before 2011, had never condemned the domestic human rights abuses of an Arab leader.[16]

The events of 2011 removed Mubarak as a stop-gap and threatened to introduce an unpredictable leadership structure in Egypt. The unleashing of the Muslim Brotherhood in Egypt and its apparent organizational strength—even before elections brought the group legislative

---

16. In a major departure from past practice, in 2011 the Arab League condemned both Libya and Syria for human rights violations before expelling the Syrian government under Bashar al-Assad from the league. In contrast, the Arab League throughout its history has primarily served as a forum for countries to pay lip service to unity while protecting their own sovereignty and security. See Michael Barnett and Etel Solingen, "Designed to fail or failure of design? The origins and legacy of the Arab League," in *Crafting Cooperation: Regional International Institutions in Comparative Perspective*, Amitav Acharya and Alastair Iain Johnston, eds., (Cambridge: Cambridge University Press, 2007) 180–220; Charles Tripp, "Regional Organizations in the Arab Middle East," in Regionalism in *World Politics*, Louise Fawcett and Andrew Hurrell, eds., 283–309 (Oxford: Oxford University Press, 1994).

and executive power—raised the possibility that political movements and ideas questioning other rulers' legitimacy and control would gain institutional strength. Islamist theories and modes of governance might soon sweep across the region. This new potential future was terrifying both to Gulf leaders and to secular elites with tepid views toward democracy across the region. Egypt was the epicenter of this potential earthquake.

The Muslim Brotherhood capitalized on the opportunity. The Freedom and Justice Party's victory in parliamentary elections in 2012 and Mohammed Morsi's presidential victory in 2013 stunned and disturbed Gulf elites. The general manager of *Al Arabiya*, for example, wrote an op-ed shortly after Morsi was sworn in wondering whether the new president could be trusted to fight terrorism and not interfere in the affairs of his neighbors.[17] Morsi himself felt it necessary to assuage Gulf leaders by pledging in his inaugural speech that he would not seek to "export revolution."[18] A strong U.S. presence in Egypt had not threatened Gulf leaders; an absent United States and the rise of alternative forces in Egypt did.

Since then, Gulf states have been at odds with the United States and with one another over how to act toward Egypt. Qatar embraced the opportunity to become the patron of Islamists in Egypt and elsewhere around the region. Saudi Arabia and the UAE took the opposite view, though at first they cautiously sought ways to work with the Morsi government while undermining the Brotherhood elsewhere. They sought to root out Brotherhood activists and activities within their own borders,[19] and they later responded with glee when the Brotherhood in turn was overthrown in Egypt in July 2013. According to stories told by officials in Riyadh, then-General Sisi visited King Abdullah in Saudi Arabia to seek his blessing just days before ousting Morsi. Whether or not this is true, the fact that the claim is made with pride in Saudi Arabia indicates the feeling toward Egypt.

After Sisi ousted Morsi, Saudi Arabia and the UAE poured support into Egypt, both financial and political, although the rate of new aid announcements and disbursements has been slower than many in Egypt hoped.[20] The UAE has given a $1 billion grant and a $2 billion interest-free loan to the Egyptian Central Bank while

17. Abdul Rahman al-Rashed, "What will Morsi do?" *Al Arabiya*, July 2, 2012, http://english.alarabiya.net/views/2012/07/02/223925.html.
18. Ellen Knickmeyer, "Egyptian Leader's Visit Sends Signal to Saudis," *Wall Street Journal*, July 11, 2012, http://www.wsj.com/articles/SB10001424052702303644004577520911170661298.
19. For a more detailed discussion, see Jon B. Alterman and William McCants, "Saudi Arabia: Islamists Rising and Falling," in Jon B. Alterman, ed., *Religious Radicalism after the Arab Uprisings* (Center for Strategic and International Studies, 2014), 144–175.
20. Enas Hamad, "As Gulf aid dries up, Egypt struggles," *Al Monitor*, December 30, 2014, http://www.al-monitor.com/pulse/originals/2014/12/egypt-economic-woes-continue-unfilled-promises-support.html.

allocating around $8 billion for energy and development programs.[21] The latter include projects in healthcare, transportation, education, energy, housing, and food security; technical assistance to develop new economic plans; and political support as Egypt courts additional donors and investors. Saudi Arabia initially offered Egypt $1 billion in cash, a $2 billion loan, and $2 billion in fuel products;[22] it also sent Egypt $3 billion worth of refined oil products from April to September 2014 alone.[23] Politically, Gulf governments have defended Sisi against his detractors internationally, supporting Egyptian assertions that the 2013 events were a "second revolution," that human rights in Egypt are well in hand,[24] and that what Egypt needs most right now from the international community is solidarity in the face of terrorist threats. The Gulf governments also have led efforts to persuade other donors and investors to make the same bet on Egypt that they have. In March 2015, Saudi Arabia and the UAE are partnering with Egypt to host a major conference on the economic future of Egypt, bringing together wealthy investors, companies, and government officials from all over the world. Saudi Arabia, the UAE, and Kuwait also announced they would collectively deposit a further $10 billion in Egypt's Central Bank before the conference.[26] But it is unclear how sustainable Gulf financial commitments to Egypt will be, particularly given the recent decline in oil prices. While GCC economies face no immediate dire threats from lower prices, reduced revenues could reduce their willingness to dole out bail-out funds to the Egyptian government.

For now, their efforts rest on the premise that Egypt can have an economic renaissance without liberalizing politically. Gulf governments are not interested in political liberalism in Egypt. Political liberalism brought them the Muslim Brotherhood. Their bet, instead, is that a strong Egyptian state that holds groups such as the Muslim Brotherhood in check and stamps out terrorism by any means necessary will create the necessary environment for economic growth. That, in turn, will ensure its future political stability. In the short term, they seem to aim narrowly at

---

21. UAE Ministry of Foreign Affairs, *The United Arab Emirates Foreign Assistance Program to the Arab Republic of Egypt: An Overview*, 2014.
22. "Saudi Arabia pledges $5 billion in aid to Egypt," *CBS News*, July 9, 2013, http://www.cbsnews.com/news/saudi-arabia-pledges-5-billion-in-aid-to-egypt/.
23. "Saudi Arabia sent Egypt $3 billion worth of oil since April," Reuters, September 25, 2014, http://af.reuters.com/article/egyptNews/idAFL6N0RQ1EU20140925.
24. In January, however, prominent Emirati commentator Abdulkhaleq Abdulla made waves in Egypt when he asserted that stability and repression in Egypt need not go hand in hand, and that the UAE government did not support the return of a "police state" in Egypt. See "Tabayun fi tafsir taghridat al-akadimi al-Imirati Abdulkhaleq Abdulla hawl al-'awda' fi Masr" [Varying interpretations of the Tweets of Emirati academic Abdelkhaleq Abdulla about the situation in Egypt], *CNN Arabic*, January 9, 2015, http://arabic.cnn.com/middleeast/2015/01/08/ayman-nour-egypt-uae-abdulkhaleq-abdullah.
25. "Egypt to host major economic conference in March," Associated Press, November 22, 2014, http://english.alarabiya.net/en/business/economy/2014/11/22/Egypt-to-host-major-economic-conference-in-March.html.
26. "Gulf states to deposit $10 bln in Egypt before conference," Reuters, February 4, 2015, http://uk.reuters.com/article/2015/02/04/egypt-gulf-investment-idUKL6N0VE2RU20150204.

preventing Egypt from falling off an economic cliff, which could precipitate a political crisis that would bring down Egypt's new political order.

It is with respect to the future of political Islamism that the Gulf states may have more specific agendas for Egypt in mind. Gulf leaders now identify the Muslim Brotherhood, Iran, and radical jihadi groups such as the Islamic State group (ISG) as the core threats to their security. Confronting the former has become a centerpiece of their approach to the rest of the Middle East. The UAE and Saudi Arabia have declared the Muslim Brotherhood a terrorist organization and prosecuted some individuals believed to be affiliated with the Brotherhood, while others have been intimidated into silence.[27] Even if the Brotherhood does not actually represent the existential threat that Gulf states portray, it serves both Egypt and the Gulf as a convenient scapegoat and bogeyman against which they can rally national sentiment and justify security measures.

Even if the Brotherhood does not actually represent the existential threat that Gulf states portray, it serves both Egypt and the Gulf as a convenient scapegoat and bogeyman.

As they have done at home, Saudi Arabia and the UAE may seek to promote in Egypt a model of apolitical Islamism that promotes piety, observance, and conservative social mores (more strictly in the case of Saudi Arabia's Wahhabi tradition) while supporting existing state structures and eschewing political activism. Such a model would not be new to Egypt: for decades, Egypt's largely apolitical salafists organized and preached throughout the country, sometimes with the encouragement of the state, as a counter-balance to the Muslim Brotherhood. Many of Egypt's salafists embraced politics following the overthrow of Mubarak, forming new political parties and participating in elections. But since the overthrow of Morsi, they have fragmented. Some support the Muslim Brotherhood as it faces persecution, others (the Nour Party) continue to embrace politics, while still others have returned to the kind of apolitical social activism and religious focus that kept them in good stead with prior Egyptian governments over the decades. Many suspect that Saudi Arabia supports Egypt's apolitical salafists financially, although with how much money and through what channels remain unclear (and Saudi officials have denied allegations about aid to Egyptian salafi groups).[28]

27. Alterman and McCants, "Saudi Arabia."

28. See for example Randa Abul Azm, "Saudi envoy to Egypt denies Kingdom offered salafis billions," *Al Arabiya*, August 1, 2011, http://english.alarabiya.net/articles/2011/08/01/160331.html.

The UAE, in contrast, is less enamored of salafists. The Emiratis are not Wahhabi, and their institutional Islam emphasizes values of stability and relative tolerance of diversity and pluralism (so long as it is not politically threatening). In this variety of Islam, good Muslims are pious, but not preachy. They observe their faith, but they do not demand that its strictest rules and regulations be enforced by law. Non-Muslim expatriates who live in the UAE are expected to respect generally conservative social norms, but may practice their own religions. Reportedly, Morocco—with UAE support—is beginning to work with both Tunisia and Egypt on mosque reform and imam training projects designed to boost a version of "moderate Islam" that can more readily compete with salafi and jihadi ideologies.[29] The UAE also established a new institution in 2014, the Muslim Council of Elders, to support efforts to "extinguish the fires that sweep across the region and address the evils of sectarianism and violence plaguing the Muslim world.[30]

President Sisi seems the perfect portrait of apolitical faith in power.

In this light, President Sisi is an important ally on not only a political front, but an ideological one. He seems the perfect portrait of apolitical faith in power. He is widely regarded as pious. When he was first raised to the position of head of the SCAF under Morsi, many speculated that it was because he held conservative religious views that the Brotherhood appreciated.[31] But he does not cite his faith as the justification for his mode of governance. Sisi has supported new efforts to reform and revitalize Azhar as a counterweight to both Muslim Brotherhood and salafi ideologies. At the beginning of 2015, he spoke both at Azhar[32] and at one of Egypt's largest Christian churches during a mass for Coptic Christmas[33] to deliver dual messages of religious moderation and harmony. He chided Azhar scholars to modernize their thinking and find ways to combat the world's image of Muslims as

29. Morocco has been implementing efforts to promote moderate Maliki Islam as a counterweight to salafi radicalism for more than a decade and appears now to be interested in exporting its model to other countries in the region.
30. Samir Salama, "Muslim Council of Elders set up in Abu Dhabi," *Gulf News*, July 20, 2014, http://gulfnews.com/news/gulf/uae/government/muslim-council-of-elders-set-up-in-abu-dhabi-1.1361897.
31. In Egypt, many even referred to him as "the Brotherhood's man" inside SCAF, while others scoffed at this suggestion, seeing Sisi as a paragon of "moderate" Islam in contrast to the Brotherhood. See Ahmed Fouad, "Bil-tawarikh: rihlat al-Sisi min ragul al-Ikhwan fi 2012 hata 'aduw al-Gama'a fi 2013" [In dates: Sisi's journey from "the Brotherhood's man" in 2012 to "enemy of the Brotherhood" in 2013], *Al Shorouk*, December 31, 2013, http://www.shorouknews.com/news/view.aspx?cdate=31122013&id=d81fbb74-3922-40d6-85ed-2ccf33343544; Yasser Rizq, "The General Sisi I Know," trans. Tyler Huffman, *Al Monitor*, July 28, 2013, http://www.al-monitor.com/pulse/politics/2013/07/sisi-egypt-morsi-ouster.html.
32. "Sisi at the celebration of the Prophet's *mawlid:* There are holy religious texts that antagonize the whole world...we need a religious revolution," [Arabic], YouTube, uploaded January 1, 2015, https://www.youtube.com/watch?v=8igW9aM4Jzg&feature=youtu.be.
33. "On video...Sisi: It was necessary that I attend the Christmas mass...and we will build the country together," [Arabic], YouTube, uploaded January 6, 2015, https://www.youtube.com/watch?v=8YidleIQjwk.

violent and extreme. He assured Christians that Egyptians were one people (some in Egypt and abroad criticized these performances as disingenuous efforts to burnish his image). Some foreign observers taken with these efforts hailed Sisi as a potential "Muslim Martin Luther."[34]

Whether Sisi can actually effect Islamic reform from his current position (and given his military rather than scholastic background) is questionable. But for those opposed to the Muslim Brotherhood and its sociopolitical goals, he is the new standard-bearer for a contrasting vision of how to combine religion and politics. In the coming years, there may be some competition between Saudi Arabia and the UAE in Egypt with respect to the particular varieties of Islam they support, rhetorically and financially. But both are likely to get behind any version that preaches the dangers of political Islam and the destructiveness of rebellion.

EGYPT'S AGENDA: DIVERSIFY SUPPORT FOR DOMESTIC STABILITY

As the Gulf states look toward Egypt to secure their stability, Egypt itself has taken steps to establish its own foreign policy priorities and demonstrate its will to act within its neighborhood. To be sure, for the moment domestic security and stability remain paramount. Quelling ongoing protests by Muslim Brotherhood members, disappointed revolutionaries, and others while combating rising jihadi violence in the Sinai Peninsula and Libya come first. Egypt has had very limited involvement with the conflicts in Syria and Iraq, and it has had little to do with its Gulf patrons' regional confrontation with Iran through proxy wars and battles from Lebanon to Yemen.

But the drive for security at home has had a ripple effect on relations with other nations in the region. Egypt's suppression of the Muslim Brotherhood has driven a rift in its relations with Turkey and Qatar, although the latter has recently pursued a rapprochement with Egypt as part of a reconciliation among the Gulf Cooperation Council states.[35] The quest for domestic security has also affected Egypt's relationships with Libya and Ethiopia.

Egypt's airstrikes on groups reportedly affiliated with the ISG (which beheaded 21 Egyptian Copts in a gruesome video released in February 2015) represented the culmination of more than a year of escalating Egyptian opposition to militancy

---

34. See for example Robert Spencer, "Egypt's Sisi calls for 'modern, comprehensive understanding of the religion of Islam,'" *Jihadwatch.org*, January 28, 2014, http://www.jihadwatch.org/2014/01/sisi-calls-for-modern-comprehensive-understanding-of-the-religion-of-islam.
35. "Egypt and Qatar take steps toward reconciliation: Saudi," *Ahram Online*, December 20, 2014, http://english.ahram.org.eg/NewsContent/1/64/118452/Egypt/Politics-/Egypt-and-Qatar-take-steps-towards-reconciliation-.aspx.

emanating from Libya. Egyptian officials repeatedly remind international observers of the threat that Libya's civil war and jihadi-salafi groups pose to Egypt's land and people. In July 2014, 21 Egyptian soldiers were killed in an attack on a border checkpoint with Libya.[36] Militants in Tripoli have also attacked the Egyptian and UAE embassies.[37] Weapons from Libya reportedly travel through Egypt to the Sinai, helping to arm militant groups there. Instability in Libya also means that the estimated hundreds of thousands of Egyptians who work in Libya face economic distress, dislocation, and violence.[38] The Egyptians murdered in the February video had been captured in early January,[39] and dozens of other Egyptians have been held hostage or killed by militant groups over the past few years.[40] In response, before it began openly attacking purported ISG militants in parts of Libya, Egypt had reportedly been providing assistance to Libyan General Khalifa Heftar's Operation Dignity movement in coordination with the UAE for months. In February, in addition to dropping bombs on Libya, Sisi called on countries in the region to create a joint Arab military force to contain the threat from the ISG and said that the UAE and Jordan had already volunteered to aid Egypt in Libya.[41]

Negotiations over the Renaissance Dam project in Ethiopia have also become a top Egyptian foreign policy priority. Under the Morsi government, Egyptian rhetoric toward Ethiopia aggravated relations between the two countries, particularly after a meeting was broadcast showing cabinet officials vowing they would attack Ethiopia if the dam project went forward.[42] Since Sisi took over, Egypt has participated in multiple multilateral dialogue sessions about the dam, and high-profile diplomatic visits have taken place between Egypt and Ethiopia. President Sisi visited Addis Ababa in January 2015 to smooth relations (though his trip was cut short by a major attack in the Sinai). At the begin-

---

36. "Egypt vows to punish attackers in border checkpoint assault," Agence France-Presse, July 20, 2014, http://english.alarabiya.net/en/News/middle-east/2014/07/20/Egypt-vows-to-punish-attackers-in-border-checkpoint-assault-.html.
37. "Embassies of Egypt and UAE attacked in Libya," *Al Jazeera*, November 13, 2014, http://www.aljazeera.com/news/middleeast/2014/11/embassies-egypt-uae-attacked-libya-201411137319239874.html.
38. There is no reliable count of how many Egyptians are in Libya. Before 2011, the International Organization for Migration estimated that between 330,000 and 1.5 million Egyptians were working in Libya. Some have since left, but other Egyptians seeking work have continued to travel to Libya even amid instability there. After the beheading video was released in February 2015, Egyptian government officials estimated that between 500,000 and 800,000 Egyptians were in Libya. "Ministry: 800,000 Egyptian workers in Libya," *Egypt Independent*, February 25, 2015, http://www.egyptindependent.com/news/ministry-800000-egyptian-workers-libya.
39. "Isis claims abduction of 21 Christians in Libya," Agence France-Presse, January 12, 2015, http://www.theguardian.com/world/2015/jan/12/isis-abducts-christians-libya-egypt.
40. See for example Ahmad Mustafa, "Egyptians reluctant to leave Libya," *Al Monitor*, September 15, 2014, http://www.al-monitor.com/pulse/politics/2014/09/egyptians-libya-border-security.html; "Update: Attempting to flee Libya, 17 Egyptians killed while at Tunisian border," *MadaMasr*, July 31, 2014, http://www.madamasr.com/news/update-attempting-flee-libya-17-egyptians-killed-while-waiting-tunisian-border.
41. "Egypt's El Sisi calls for joint Arab military force," *National*, February 23, 2015, http://www.thenational.ae/world/middle-east/egypts-el-sisi-calls-for-joint-arab-military-force.
42. Liam Stack, "With Cameras Rolling, Egyptian Politicians Threaten Ethiopia Over Dam," *New York Times*, June 6, 2013, http://thelede.blogs.nytimes.com/2013/06/06/with-cameras-rolling-egyptian-politicians-threaten-ethiopia-over-dam/.

ning of March, the countries involved in debate over the dam—Egypt, Ethiopia, and Sudan—reportedly reached a preliminary new agreement over how to manage use of the Nile's water.[43] While Egyptian officials continue to express concerns about what the dam will mean for Egypt's water security, they seem committed to addressing the challenge through quiet diplomacy rather than bombast.

> *The United States has a different strategic view from the Gulf states of what it will require to set Egypt on a stable, sustainable path. But Washington has neither the political will nor leverage to press its point.*

The future of Egypt's relationships with global powers—the United States, China, Russia, and the European Union—is less certain. Sisi made his first official visit to China in late 2014. His goal is to strengthen Sino-Egyptian ties into a "strategic partnership" that aims to raise significant Chinese investment in Egypt and allow Egypt to purchase Chinese arms.[44] Sisi has also pursued warmer ties with Russia. Egypt concluded a deal with Russia in 2014 to purchase $3.5 billion in weaponry;[45] earlier discussions of the deal indicated it would be funded by Saudi Arabia and the UAE.[46] In addition, in February Egypt concluded a $5.9 billion arms deal with France to buy 24 Rafale fighter jets.[47] Egypt's relationships with the EU and with individual European countries have followed roughly the same trajectory as its relationship with the United States. The Europeans have condemned human rights abuses in Egypt and pressured it to create a genuinely open, liberal democracy. But they have not significantly cut their aid to Egypt, which, unlike U.S. aid, is concentrated more in

---

43. Campbell MacDiarmid, "Hydro diplomacy on the Nile," *Al Jazeera*, March 10, 2015, http://www.aljazeera.com/news/2015/03/hydro-diplomacy-nile-150309092540029.html.
44. "China, Egypt elevate bilateral relationship to comprehensive strategic partnership," Xinhua, December 23, 2014, http://news.xinhuanet.com/english/china/2014-12/23/c_133874597.htm.
45. "Russia, Egypt seal preliminary arms deal worth $3.5 billion: agency," Reuters, September 21, 2014, http://www.reuters.com/article/2014/09/17/us-russia-egypt-arms-idUSKBN0HC19T20140917.
46. Maggie Michael, "Egypt military chief heads to Moscow in rare visit," Associated Press, February 12, 2014, http://bigstory.ap.org/article/drive-shooting-egypt-kills-3-policemen.
47. "Egypt, France to sign €5.2 billion deal for Rafale Jets," *France24*, February 16, 2015, http://www.france24.com/en/20150216-france-egypt-sign-deal-sale-rafale-fighter-jets/.

economic and social development programs than military assistance.[48]

The United States faces a dilemma in formulating its policy toward Egypt. It has a different strategic view from the Gulf states of what it will require to set Egypt on a stable, sustainable path. But Washington has neither the political will nor leverage to press its point. The United States continues to stress that Egypt needs to be on a path to democracy. Washington implies that economic resurgence in Egypt will be difficult without political liberalization—or at least a more benign application of autocratic rule against liberal dissidents than Sisi currently demonstrates. Economic success will be hard under any circumstances for a country of 90 million people with few comparative advantages. Egypt has a large youth population with skills mismatched to the labor market, an environment that hinders entrepreneurship, a dysfunctional educational system, and a corrupt public sector dominated by the very institution, the military, which the president seeks to protect and empower. It is not a recipe for turning Egypt into a new South Korea or even Vietnam. While the Gulf states' theory is that Egypt can grow its way to stability, the United States and others remain doubtful that Egypt can weather the inevitable economic challenges it will face under a political system that remains repressive in the face of even non-violent dissent and criticism. But they cannot or will not do much about that for now.

Tantalizingly for Egypt, the current situation offers it the prospect of keeping the goods it gets from the United States while being less reliant on it overall.

At the moment, Egypt's relationship with the United States is an ambivalent one on both sides: coordination and cooperation continue, but tensions are high and rhetoric often sharp. For Egypt, this ambivalence serves domestic purposes in the current environment. Maligning and blaming the United States for current or past problems in Egypt plays to long-standing anti-U.S. sentiment in Egypt and to deeper currents of resentment, anxiety, and paranoia. Fear of foreign domination that threatens

48. In August 2013, the EU outlined concrete steps that it would take in response to continued state violence in Egypt, announcing that EU members would "suspend export licenses to Egypt of any equipment which might be used in internal repression," "review their security assistance with Egypt," and assess the continued provision of non-security aid as events developed. Yet no immediate aid cuts were announced at that time. The EU had already cut direct budget assistance to Egypt, most EU aid was not security-related, and aid provision had already slowed greatly in 2013. As Sisi consolidated his control in 2014, the EU made increasingly strident criticisms of his government while continuing to slowly release non-security aid to the country. France also concluded a 1 billion euro deal to sell four naval frigates to Egypt in July 2014. Council of the European Union: Press Release, August 21, 2013, http://www.consilium.europa.eu/uedocs/cms_Data/docs/pressdata/EN/foraff/138603.pdf; Justyna Pawlak and John O'Donnell, "EU shies away from cutting aid for Egypt," Reuters, August 21, 2013, http://www.reuters.com/article/2013/08/21/us-egypt-protests-eu-idUSBRE97K0WE20130821; "News: Egypt," *EU Neighbourhood Info Centre*, http://www.enpi-info.eu/list_type_med.php?&country=2&search=1&id_type=1; "France secures 1 billion euro navy deal in Egypt," Reuters, July 19, 2014, http://english.alarabiya.net/en/News/middle-east/2014/07/19/France-secures-1-billion-euro-navy-deal-in-Egypt.html.

to weaken, undermine, or split the Egyptian state has been a common feature of public rhetoric in Egypt for much of its modern history. Feeling aggrieved at the machinations of foreign powers helps rally people together in defense of Egypt. The public has no trouble believing rumors that Hillary Clinton admitted the United States helped create the Islamic State group (ISG) or that former Ambassador Anne Patterson schemed to help keep the Muslim Brotherhood in power by bringing fighters into Egypt from Gaza.[49]

But maintaining a somewhat positive relationship with the United States also serves the Egyptian government's purposes: it can continue to receive $1.3 billion in aid, intelligence assistance, military training, trade, and investment in exchange for allowing the U.S. military overflight authorization and priority passage through the Suez Canal while keeping the peace with Israel. The latter task involves efforts to combat Hamas and jihadi-salafi militancy in Gaza and the Sinai, efforts which are also in the Egyptian government's interest for its domestic security. Tantalizingly for Egypt, the current situation offers it the prospect of keeping the goods it gets from the United States while being less reliant on it overall because Egypt can now also turn to the Gulf, to Russia, to France, and to China to try to balance its U.S. relationship. Egypt is still using its foreign policy to support its domestic politics and security—but its support network is more diverse than it was before 2011.

A NEW ROLE FOR EGYPT?

That support network is split, however, between those with a desire to see Egypt "succeed" by establishing a genuinely democratic political system and sustainable economic path and those who think the economic success might be achieved without democracy. The Gulf's economic salvage operation represents the latter approach. Their efforts may keep Egypt's economy from imploding, but economic largesse cannot mend or strengthen state-society relations that the events of the past few years and continued authoritarian repression have deeply damaged.

Considering Egypt's future, then, it is important to ask not only what will happen if these efforts are not enough and Egypt does "fail," but also what will happen if Egypt muddles through. That is, what can we expect to see if Gulf and other aid keeps Egypt afloat, but not so much that it can transform itself into a country less dependent on outside support? Will Egypt then remain focused on internal stability and politics, avoiding involvement in regional issues except where the challenges directly concern Egypt's stability and security, as in Libya? Or will Sisi—or whoever follows him—grow more assertive and seek to articulate a new version of Egyptian regional leadership? That leadership could be relatively indepen-

---

49. Robert Mackey, "Borne by Facebook, Conspiracy Theory That U.S. Created ISIS Spreads Across Middle East," *New York Times*, August 26, 2014, http://www.nytimes.com/2014/08/27/world/middleeast/isis-conspiracy-theories-include-a-purported-american-plot.html?_r=0; Ursula Lindsey, "The Tall Tales of Cairo," *New York Times*, August 29, 2013, http://latitude.blogs.nytimes.com/2013/08/29/the-tall-tales-of-cairo/.

dent, but it is more likely to align with the approaches of Saudi Arabia and the UAE.

In the coming years we might see all three countries working together to propagate and uphold their vision of apolitical but pious Islamic societies, banded together by the narrative that only they can hold back a jihadi deluge. After decades of Egypt as first the revolutionary beacon of the Middle East and then as the U.S.-aligned lame duck of the Middle East, we may be moving to a new configuration, one in which Egypt is a partner with the Gulf in a new regional order that embraces controlled economic liberalization, autocratic political order, apolitical Islamic conservatism, and an ambivalent relationship with the United States. The United States and others will need to decide what kind of relationship they want to have, not just with each country individually, but with this new regional political framework. ■

9 The Arab-Israeli Conflict

GHAITH AL-OMARI

For the last seven decades, the Israeli-Palestinian conflict has been a central defining feature of the Middle Eastern geostrategic landscape. In recent years, resolving this conflict through a negotiated two-state solution has become a matter of global and regional consensus and the subject of numerous initiatives. Changing realities between and within Palestine and Israel and the transformations facing the region at large have raised questions as to the feasibility of reaching such a permanent solution.

The question of whether negotiations can resolve the conflict and create an independent Palestinian state has led some to indifference and others to renewed zeal. Ironically, as some regional forces appear to be drifting toward distancing themselves from the Israeli-Palestinian conflict, several European governments are deepening their engagement on the issue with a more critical stance toward Israel.

Both approaches—indifference and engagement—could precipitate a dramatic shift from the status quo. Actions such as UN Security Council (UNSC) recognition of Palestinian statehood, Israeli annexation of West Bank territory, or the collapse of the Palestinian Authority (PA) could lead the conflict into a new phase with potentially profound diplomatic and political consequences. A series of resultant events could dislodge the presumed U.S. mediating role, create a new arena of violent conflict in a region already in turmoil, and lock Israelis and Palestinians into another round of sustained violence which would exact large economic, political, and human tolls.

PROSPECTS FOR ISRAELI-PALESTINIAN PEACE

Currently, the prospects for a resolution to the Israeli-Palestinian conflict seem slim. While still desiring a two-state solution, Israeli public opinion has largely abandoned the hope of reaching a permanent peace agreement. Israelis widely believe there is no partner on the Palestinian side with the political will or muscle to negotiate a peace agreement. The Israeli national security establishment's priorities are Iran's nuclear program, ongoing regional changes, and terrorism. The lack of prospects for peace, along with the government's right-leaning world view, has placed Israel at odds with much of the international community. That includes close allies such as the United States and much of Europe. A combination of all these factors has created a sense of defensiveness and uncertainty, hardening Israeli positions.

> *Arab uncertainty about U.S. leadership, intentions, and dependability casts its shadow on the prospects for robust regional support for pursuing Israeli-Palestinian peace.*

The Palestinian arena is no less complicated. In a striking mirror image of Israeli public opinion, most Palestinians desire a two-state solution but see it as unachievable because of the lack of an Israeli partner. And Palestinian politics are paralyzed. A deep divide remains between Hamas, which has ruled Gaza since violently taking it over in 2007, and Fatah, which dominates the Palestine Liberation Organization (PLO) and the Palestinian Authority (PA) West Bank government. Successive attempts to recreate national unity have collapsed in all but name. Hamas and Fatah each face a crisis of legitimacy due to their lack of a credible national vision to establish an independent state, perceptions of their corruption and poor governance, and restrictions on public freedoms. For Fatah—and by extension the PLO and the PA—the question of succession looms large and largely unanswered. In the meantime, the Palestinian arena is becoming again the theater for regional proxy power play, as seen in last summer's Gaza war.

Regionally, the Palestinian issue appears much less pressing. The Arab world is preoccupied with other regional priorities: Iran's nuclear program and wider regional role; the fallout of the Arab uprisings in Egypt, Syria, Iraq, Yemen, and elsewhere; and the Islamic State group (ISG) and violent extremism. Additionally, Arab uncertainty about U.S. leadership, intentions, and dependability casts its shadow on the prospects for robust regional support for pursuing Israeli-Palestinian peace. Common threats facing Arab states and Israel have intensified their already-existing yet unacknowledged security relations. But these relations have been unable to cross over to diplomacy and other forms of overt cooperation due to the lack of progress on the peace process.

After two costly failed attempts at peacemaking during the Barack Obama administration, the United States seems reluctant to try again. Even if the administration were inclined to reengage or reassess its policy, as President Obama has indicated following Prime Minister Benjamin Netanyahu's election eve dismissal of a Palestinian state, it will have to contend with more immediate regional priorities. Negotiations regarding Iran's nuclear program continue to create domestic and international challenges. In the meantime, building and maintaining a broad international coalition for the campaign in Iraq and Syria against the ISG demands significant attention.

All these factors—from the Palestinian side, the Israeli side, the region, and the United States—combine to make successful negotiations unlikely in the short term. The continuation of the status quo seems to be the most likely scenario going forward, even as many international leaders suggest that the status quo is unsustainable—or at least potentially disruptive.

IMPLICATIONS FOR PALESTINE

The continuation of the status quo raises challenges for Israel, the Palestinians, and the region. These challenges are perhaps most severe for the Palestinians by virtue of the transitional nature of the PA and the Palestinians' lack of sovereignty. For the Palestinians, the continuation of the status quo means the continuation of the occupation, with all its attendant social, material, and political hardships.

Diplomatic Crisis

The lack of progress toward ending the occupation has put tremendous strain on Palestinian political and governance institutions. The PLO, the PA, and Fatah have invested all their credibility in the quest to reach a negotiated two-state solution. With that prospect receding, the leadership finds itself directionless and unable to present a vision around which Palestinians can rally.

The PLO leadership has sought to divert some of the pressure through a series of diplomatic steps such as joining international treaties and UN agencies, seeking bilateral recognition from states, and resorting to the UNSC to recognize Palestinian statehood. While such steps are popular and have temporarily buttressed the PA's domestic standing, this approach presents significant risks. Most important, this approach cannot produce concrete changes in the reality on the ground. It cannot deliver economic breakthroughs that would mollify the Palestinian public by improving people's day-to-day lives. Instead, for this approach to continue generating traction, it must assume an escalatory dynamic: after each step that fails to change reality, the PA will have to take a more severe measure to grab its public's imagination. This presents two problems. First, there is a finite number of measures at the Palestinians' disposal. Indeed, once the Palestinians have joined the International Criminal Court (ICC), there remain few if any further meaningful diplomatic steps that they can take. Second, as the Palestinian steps increase in severity, so would the Israeli and potentially U.S. reaction. In response to Palestine joining the ICC, Israel has withheld transfer of tax revenues to the PA. Steps are under way in the U.S. Congress to defund the PA as well.

National Disunity

Other factors beyond the PA-Hamas rift exacerbate the strain on the Palestinians: the lack of progress on Gaza reconstruction and Palestinian governing institutions' inability to build legitimacy based on good governance and representative politics.

Ending the division between Palestinian factions has consistently topped the domestic priorities of the Palestinian public. The June 2014 Palestinian "government of national consensus" is the latest in a string of failed reconciliation initiatives. Reconciliation is complicated by both the ongoing struggle between the Muslim Brotherhood and key Arab governments, particularly Egypt, and the "Quartet conditions" which would automatically isolate any government in which Hamas takes part. Internal factors, including the sets of vested interests that Hamas and Fatah have developed in their respective areas of control and tensions within Fatah itself between its national leadership and its Gaza base, further complicate reconciliation.

A unity government is only one—and the easiest—component of Palestinian national reconciliation. Previous reconciliation attempts have failed to find satisfactory solutions for the wide gap in ideology between the two sides. A proposed "leadership framework," which will have an advisory capacity to the PLO without actually being part of the organization, will deal with the immediate challenge posed by the two parties' irreconcilable ideology. But as long as this question remains unresolved, the ideological gap will consistently pose challenges to decision-making and unity.

Even if problems relating to ideology, vested interests, and other considerations could be resolved, Hamas's unwillingness to disband its military wing makes any political reconciliation inherently unstable. The high degree of decisionmaking autonomy Hamas's military wing enjoys means it will always have the option to exert its independence vis-à-vis Hamas's political leadership, to directly pressure the PA in cases of political stalemate, or to reignite a conflict with Israel to completely reshuffle the deck.

> *The high degree of decisionmaking autonomy Hamas's military wing enjoys means it will always have the option to exert its independence vis-à-vis Hamas's political leadership.*

Given these considerations, national disunity is likely to continue. The continued division has harmed the political credibility of both Hamas and Fatah. Opinion polls show a steadily growing number of Palestinians believing that the two parties favor narrow partisan interests over national ones. This comes on top of already shaky credibility of both groups due to systemic repression of political dissent and the corruption and bad governance that have marred their rule in their respective territories.

Bad Governance

In the West Bank, governance reforms instituted under former Prime Minister Salam Fayyad have gradually eroded. President Mahmoud Abbas stifles criticism of him or his policies not only when it originates from Hamas but also from Fatah members or independents. Abbas's term expired in 2009, and no potential successors have emerged. Fatah suffers from internal factional tensions and has been unable to hold internal elections originally scheduled for 2014.

Hamas's credibility in Gaza has not fared much better. Hamas initially was successful when it blamed economic hardships on the Israeli blockade and the isolation resulting from the Quartet's conditions. But that effort was unsustainable. Corruption and bad governance, brutal responses to any dissent, three devastating wars with Israel, and regional isolation due to Hamas's deep affiliation with the Muslim Brotherhood have undermined its legitimacy and credibility. Hamas also cannot claim to be representative on the basis of its victory in the 2006 legislative election, because the Palestinian Legislative Council's term expired in 2010.

In both the West Bank and Gaza, prospects for parliamentary or presidential elections are slim. As a result, the Palestinians have no avenues for rejuvenating their political structures. While Hamas's control over Gaza and Fatah's over the West Bank are not in immediate danger, the trend of diminishing legitimacy weakens Palestinian political and governing institutions and creates fragility and volatility.

PA Collapse?

This confluence of diplomatic and domestic crises has a profound impact on the Palestinian leadership. For the national-secular leadership, namely the PA and the PLO, this manifests itself in a narrowing margin of maneuverability when it comes to decisionmaking and in overall heightened fragility.

Due to its credibility deficit among the Palestinians, the Palestinian leadership is ill-equipped to make major decisions that are unpopular. This immediately precludes its ability to make the necessary concessions to reach a peace deal. Instead, it will be under constant pressure to make decisions that placate the public. The most obvious are symbolic moves such as the ones taken in the United Nations and other international organizations. Parallel to that, the PA will be under constant pressure to stop unpopular policies, most notably security cooperation with Israel. Severing security cooperation with Israel will have grave repercussions. Accordingly, senior Palestinian decisionmakers are not eager to take such a step. However, following the decisions by various PLO bodies to that effect, pressure will only build on the PA. Absent political strength to withstand such pressure, a moment could come when the PA will have to stop security cooperation.

The erosion of the PA's legitimacy, along with the increasingly crisis-laden confrontational trajectory its relations with Israel seem to be following, creates fragility when it comes to the PA's very future. The current situation is characterized by internal West Bank tensions. On the one hand are significant Palestinian, Israeli, and international interests invested in the PA's survival. On the other is a Palestinian public that increasingly sees the PA as irrelevant beyond its role in paying salaries. While this points to the likelihood of continued PA survival, it is increasingly ill-equipped to handle severe crises such as prolonged inability to pay salaries or a leadership vacuum. Collapse would not only affect the PA, but also Fatah and the PLO, both of which are so thoroughly identified with the PA that their survival in case of the latter's collapse is far from certain.

While Hamas is faring slightly better, it would struggle to pick up the pieces after a PA or PLO collapse. Its failed governance of Gaza has significantly eroded its credibility among Palestinians. It is seen to share the blame equally with Fatah for the lack of unity. It is also beset with ongoing internal tensions. In the foreseeable future, the regional dynamics are extremely hostile to Hamas on a number of levels. Even if the PA collapses in the West Bank, Hamas would be unlikely to fill the vacuum due to Israeli security activities and Jordan's lack of interest in seeing a Hamas stronghold on its immediate borders.

IMPLICATIONS FOR ISRAEL

For Israel, the status quo raises a number of questions. Most fundamentally, the question is whether Israel can maintain its Jewish and democratic nature without a two-state solution. Demographers on opposing sides of the debate hotly contest trends, data, and analysis in defense of their positions. In political terms, however, this question has become the center of the debate about the two-state solution, invoked not only by Israeli commentators but also by world leaders.

> *If Israel's current trajectory continues, Europe will intensify recent policies, including votes at the United Nations, aimed at challenging Israeli diplomacy and imposing a cost on Israel's settlement policy.*

The continuation of the status quo raises the risk of isolation for Israel. This isolation stems from three factors. The first relates to relations with the Palestinians. There is the perception, which varies among world capitals, that Israel is fully or partially responsible for the failure to reach a two-state solution as a result of its negotiation positions, behavior, and ongoing policies such as settlement activity. The second relates to nuclear negotiations with Iran. Israel's positions and rhetoric, while in keeping with sentiment in many regional capitals, is at odds with the approach of both the United States and Europe. Third, statements by senior Israeli officials, including Prime Minister Netanyahu, regarding Israel's Arab minority do not correspond to many Western nations' concept of democratic values.

If Israel's current trajectory continues, Europe will intensify recent policies, including votes at the United Nations, aimed at challenging Israeli diplomacy and imposing a cost on Israel's settlement policy. The December 2014 French effort to draft a UNSC resolution laying out parameters of a permanent status agreement is an example of such measures.

Tensions have also surfaced with the United States. While both the United States and Israel take pains to stress that these tensions do not touch the fundamentals of their relationship, continued tensions are bound to harm Israel. The political tensions and divergent policies regarding the conflict have brought into question the United States' willingness to continue automatically shielding Israel in the United Nations and other international arenas.

> *Without credible progress toward ending the occupation, the PA's ability to resist public pressure will diminish.*

While in the short term the challenges to Israel's international relations do not threaten the fundamentals of its ties with longstanding allies in Europe and the United States, these challenges can usher in a new dynamic that would have a long-term impact on Israel's interests. It must be noted, however, that shifts in Israel's international relations are a response not only to Israeli policies but also to political changes in key world capitals.

More immediately, the continuation of the status quo raises a number of security threats for Israel. The situation in Gaza remains volatile. The pattern of cyclical eruption of conflict will likely continue without a fundamental change in relations with the Palestinians.

While violence in the West Bank has so far been prevented, the situation remains fragile. Key Palestinian institutions and leaders question the PA's commitment to security cooperation with Israel. Even if elites' commitment remains, a frustrated Palestinian public has increasingly criticized security cooperation. Without credible progress toward ending the occupation, the PA's ability to resist public pressure will diminish. This increased tension creates volatility. Unpredictable and therefore unmanageable incidents could trigger new explosions of violence. In an extreme scenario, these developments could trigger the collapse of the PA, creating a political and security vacuum that is likely to draw Israel back more intensively into the West Bank.

REGIONAL AND INTERNATIONAL IMPLICATIONS

For the regional and international order, the continuation of the conflict is a constant source of strain. The bulk of the disruption from recent eruptions of violence, whether the second intifada or the three wars in Gaza, has been largely contained within the Israeli-Palestinian arena. But the continuation of the conflict demands constant management and expenditure of resources.

The conflict will continue to demand diplomatic engagement. The Palestinian approach to the UNSC in late 2014 after the collapse of the U.S.-led negotiations effort is an example of this dynamic. Valuable diplomatic time and capital were spent in managing the process, distracting from other regional priorities, and inevitably creating tensions among various members of the UNSC. Additionally, as long as the conflict continues, the prospect of integrating Israel into the region—an outcome that is desired by both Israel and many Arab governments—is minimal. The burden is often higher on regional players, particularly Egypt and Jordan. The conflict's potential to mobilize Arab publics, while recently diminished, can never be fully discounted because of the issue's symbolic resonance.

Finally, the conflict adds another set of unpredictable variables to an already complex region. In the worst-case scenario, collapse of the PA could have far-reaching regional implications.

OPTIONS

Despite the risks inherent in an unstable Israeli-Palestinian front, there are few obvious options for moving forward.

Negotiations, which in the past could have introduced a measure of stability, are not a viable option for the foreseeable future. After successive failures, negotiations as a tool for ending the conflict have lost public credibility. Israelis and Palestinians both will be skeptical of renewed negotiations. Indeed, Palestinians will view them with hostility. Backchannel negotiations, which would avoid some of the political complexities of public negotiations, will still have to contend with lack of trust among Palestinian leaders, significant substantive gaps on the most sensitive issues, and a region and a world that are too preoccupied elsewhere.

The UN-focused strategy upon which the Palestinians have embarked has inherent limitations. Any measures that require action by the UNSC or the full UN membership must win the support of at least 9 of the Council's 15 members. It must also be acceptable to the United States, which has the power to veto UNSC resolutions. In response to statements made by Prime Minister Netanyahu in his 2015 reelection campaign, the United States even signaled willingness to depart from its traditional automatic veto in support of Israel. This however is unlikely to extend to allowing the admission of Palestine to the United Nations as a full member. If indeed there is a change to UNSC voting patterns, it will likely be in relation to resolutions concerning settlements.

The Palestinians might choose to force a U.S. veto. Such a decision would not only add strain on U.S.-Palestinian relations, but it would also disturb delicate U.S.-Arab cooperation regarding myriad regional issues. Such a scenario is not favored by the United States or key Arab partners, who will likely try to dissuade the Palestinians from such a showdown. The Palestinians have an almost automatic majority in the United Nations General Assembly (UNGA), but the powers of the UNGA are limited, and arguably were exhausted when Palestine attained the status of non-member observer state at the United Nations in 2011.

The United States may opt to announce its own parameters for the contours of a permanent Israeli-Palestinian peace deal, either unilaterally or through its own UNSC resolution. Proponents of this approach argue that such parameters could politically reignite debate within the Palestinian and Israeli societies about peace. It also could be a diplomatic stroke to bring clarity to the concept of a two-state solution and renewed energy to international and regional efforts. Such an approach, however, requires the United States to rally sufficient international support for the substance of such parameters before they are announced. This will be a complicated process given the sensitivity of some of the issues at stake, including the fate of Jerusalem and Palestinian refugees and the issue of the Jewish nature of Israel. Realistic parameters that garner the requisite international support—including the essential support of Arab and Muslim nations—would be extremely difficult to draft. Additionally, there is little appetite in the region to expend political capital in support of a controversial U.S. initiative. There is great anxiety among traditional U.S. allies in the Arab world about the United States' negotiations with Iran and other regional issues. Without allaying these fears, it will be difficult for the United States to put together the requisite regional alliance.

The United States will need to make it clear to the Israelis and Palestinians—both of whom have grown used to ignoring the United States without much cost—that outright rejection of these ideas would trigger meaningful consequences. Failure to communicate this clearly and credibly could produce a stillborn initiative that would further diminish U.S. standing in the region. Rather than enshrining the parameters of a two state-solution, a failed effort might push the parties and their supporters toward adopting even more uncompromising public postures and in doing so further erode the beleaguered two-state solution.

Absent immediate realistic options for a conflict-ending initiative, there are some steps that can be taken on the ground to deescalate. Measures such as regular transfers of tax revenues collected by Israel on behalf of the PA, increased Palestinian access to construction and economic activities in Area "C," and other economic measures can be undertaken, especially if there is a concerted international push. These measures are no replacement for a political solution and cannot in themselves resolve the conflict. They can, however, temporarily release some of the tension on the ground and deescalate for a time until more auspicious diplomatic and political circumstances are in place.

Regardless of movement on the diplomatic track, action can also be taken to resume the reform efforts in the PA. In addition to the prospect of better services for the Palestinian public, dealing with issues of PA corruption, inefficiency, and bad governance can bring about an increased measure of legitimacy and stability to the institution.

CONCLUSION

Israeli-Palestinian dynamics are at one of their worst phases in recent memory. Bilateral issues, internal factors in both polities, a complex regional reality, and challenges facing U.S. policy and leadership dim the prospect of a conflict-ending, two-state solution. These factors have unleashed a pattern of rapidly intensifying political and diplomatic confrontations, and the situation on the ground is deteriorating. These trends can have negative implications for the Palestinians and Israelis and can have ripple effects in the region and beyond. Until a meaningful resumption of the peace process becomes possible, steps can be taken to manage the conflict. But even such measures cannot eliminate the potential for a strategic shift in prevailing dynamics which undermines the regional and global consensus that has promoted a negotiated settlement for more than three decades—a shift that could be disastrously destabilizing for the Israelis, the Palestinians, and the region. ■

About the Authors

JON B. ALTERMAN is a senior vice president, holds the Zbigniew Brzezinski Chair in Global Security and Geostrategy, and is director of the Middle East Program at CSIS. Prior to joining CSIS in 2002, he served as a member of the Policy Planning Staff at the U.S. Department of State and as a special assistant to the assistant secretary of state for Near Eastern affairs. He is a member of the Chief of Naval Operations Executive Panel and served as an expert adviser to the Iraq Study Group (also known as the Baker-Hamilton Commission). In addition to his policy work, he teaches Middle Eastern studies at the Johns Hopkins School of Advanced International Studies. Before entering government, he was a scholar at the U.S. Institute of Peace and at the Washington Institute for Near East Policy. He received his Ph.D. in history from Harvard University.

CAROLYN BARNETT is a research fellow with the Middle East Program at CSIS. Her primary research interests are in the politics, economics, and society of North Africa and the Gulf states. She also supports the Middle East Program's projects related to changing relations between Asia and the Middle East. Prior to joining CSIS, Barnett earned an M.Sc. in Middle East politics and an M.A. in Islamic studies from the School of Oriental and African Studies in London, where she studied as a Marshall scholar. She also spent a year as a graduate fellow in the Center for Arabic Study Abroad program at the American University in Cairo on a Fulbright scholarship. Barnett holds a B.S.F.S. from the School of Foreign Service at Georgetown University and is a former editor-in-chief of the Georgetown Journal of International Affairs.

STEPHEN D. BIDDLE is professor of political science and international affairs at George Washington University (GWU). He is also adjunct senior fellow at the Council on Foreign Relations where he was previously the Roger Hertog Senior Fellow for Defense Policy. He has served on the Defense Policy Board, on General David Petraeus's Joint Strategic Assessment Team in Baghdad in 2007, on General Stanley McChrystal's Initial Strategic Assessment Team in Kabul in 2009, and as a senior advisor to General Petraeus's Central Command Assessment Team in Washington in 2008-2009. Biddle has lectured and written extensively on national security policy, military strategy, and technology in modern warfare, including the award winning book *Military Power: Explaining Victory and Defeat in Modern Battle* (Princeton University Press, 2004). He earned his Ph.D. in public policy from Harvard University.

FARIDEH FARHI is affiliate graduate faculty at the University of Hawaii at Manoa. She has taught comparative politics at the University of Colorado, Boulder, University of Hawaii, University of Tehran, and Shahid Beheshti University, Tehran. Her publications include *States and Urban-Based Revolutions in Iran and Nicaragua* (University of Illinois Press) and numerous articles and book chapters on comparative analyses of revolutions and Iranian politics and foreign policy. She has been a public policy scholar at the Woodrow Wilson International Center for Scholars and consultant to the World Bank and the International Crisis Group.

HAIM MALKA is a senior fellow and deputy director of the Middle East Program at CSIS, where he oversees the program's work on the Maghreb. His principal areas of research include religious radicalization, government strategies to combat extremism, violent non-state actors, and North African politics and security. He also covers political Islam and the Arab-Israeli conflict. Before joining CSIS in 2005, he was a research analyst at the Saban Center for Middle East Policy at the Brookings Institution, where he concentrated on U.S. Middle East foreign policy. Malka spent six years living in Jerusalem, where he worked as a television news producer. He is the coauthor of *Arab Reform and Foreign Aid: Lessons from Morocco* (CSIS, 2006) and the author of *Crossroads: The Future of the U.S.-Israel Strategic Partnership* (CSIS, 2011). He holds a B.A. from the University of Washington in Seattle and an M.A. from Columbia University's School of International and Public Affairs.

JOHN MCLAUGHLIN served as deputy director of the Central Intelligence Agency from 2000-2004 and acting director from July-September 2004. He is now distinguished practitioner-in-residence at the Philip Merrill Center for Strategic Studies at the Johns Hopkins School of Advanced International Studies (SAIS), where he teaches and writes on a wide variety of foreign affairs topics. He is also a nonresident senior fellow in the Center for 21st Century Security and Intelligence at the Brookings Institution. He serves on the Central Intelligence Agency's external advisory board. He led a review of counterterrorism "lessons learned" in 2010 at the request of the director of National Intelligence. He has previously held the positions of deputy director for intelligence, vice chairman for estimates, and acting chairman of the National Intelligence Council. He founded the Sherman Kent School for Intelligence Analysis, an institution dedicated to teaching the history, mission, and essential skills of the analytic profession to new CIA employees. He serves on the Board of Trustees at the Noblis Corporation and is a member of the Council on Foreign Relations and the American Academy of Diplomacy. He holds an M.A. in international relations from SAIS.

GHAITH AL-OMARI is a senior fellow at The Washington Institute for Near East Policy and the former executive director of the American Task Force on Palestine. Previously, he served in various positions within the Palestinian Authority, including as advisor to former Prime Minister Mahmoud Abbas and as director of the international relations department in the Office of the President. He also served as an advisor to the Palestinian negotiating team throughout the permanent status negotiations with Israel from 1999 to 2001. After the breakdown of the peace talks, he was the lead Palestinian drafter of the Geneva Initiative, an unofficial model peace agreement negotiated between leading Palestinian and Israeli public figures. Omari is a lawyer by training and a graduate of Georgetown and Oxford Universities.

ROGER OWEN is the A.J. Meyer Professor of Middle East History, Emeritus at Harvard University and was previously the director of the university's Center for Middle Eastern Studies. Prior to teaching at Harvard, he was a faculty member at Oxford University, where he served several times as the director of the Saint Antony's College Middle East Centre. His books include *Cotton and the Egyptian Economy, 1820-1914* (1969), *The Middle East in the World Economy, 1800-1914* (1981), *State, Power and Politics in the Making of the Modern Middle East* (1992), *Lord Cromer: Victorian Imperialist, Edwardian Proconsul* (2004) and, with Sevket Pamuk, *A History of the Middle East Economies in the Twentieth Century* (1999).

PAUL SALEM is vice president for policy and research at The Middle East Institute (MEI). He focuses on issues of political change, democratic transition, and conflict, with a regional emphasis on the countries of the Levant and Egypt. Salem writes regularly in the Arab and Western press and has been published in numerous journals and newspapers. Prior to joining MEI, Salem was the founding director of the Carnegie Middle East Center in Beirut, Lebanon from 2006-2013. From 1999 to 2006, he was director of the Fares Foundation and in 1989 founded and directed the Lebanese Center for Policy Studies, Lebanon's leading public policy think tank.

www.ingramcontent.com/pod-product-compliance
Ingram Content Group UK Ltd.
Pitfield, Milton Keynes, MK11 3LW, UK
UKHW051419150926
475561UK00005B/242

9 781442 240964